HERITAGE BUILDERS
PUBLISHING

DOUBLE-SOUL

DOUBLE-SOUL

The true story of a preacher's secret double-life
of sexual addiction and shame.

···

GABRIEL RIVERA

with
Dr. Brad Weniger

All Scripture is taken from the King James Version (1611) of the Bible.
Any discrepancy is entirely unintentional.

HERITAGE BUILDERS PUBLISHING
MONTEREY, CLOVIS CALIFORNIA

HERITAGE BUILDERS PUBLISHING
©2015 by Gabe Rivera

First Edition 2015

Contributing Editor, Lydia Kantor
Cover Design, Ashley Dondlinger
Book Design, Keith Bennett
Published by Heritage Builders Publishing
Clovis, Monterey California 93619
www.HeritageBuilders.com   1-888-898-9563

ISBN: 978-1-942603-05-4

Printed and bound in the United States of America.

HERITAGE BUILDERS
PUBLISHING

JUDE 22

And of some have compassion,
making a difference:

DOUBLE-SOUL

Foreword

"I did not know how to say NO!"

That is the very frank and completely candid testimony of my brother in Christ, Gabriel Rivera - the author of *Double-Soul*.

It is the story of a man - a preacher - who didn't just struggle with the lust of the flesh, the lust of the eyes, and the pride of life.

He was enslaved by it. He was entrapped by it.

More than that, he was imprisoned by it.

In *Double-Soul* Gabriel Rivera Biblically and very practically calls others in this penitentiary to repentance, to purity, to accountability, and to intimacy with the Lord.

For Gabriel Rivera, it seemed there was no hope.

Double-Soul loudly and victoriously announces to men and women who do not know how to say no that there IS hope in Jesus Christ!

Attorney David Gibbs, Jr.
Christian Law Association

DOUBLE-SOUL

Dedication

This book is prayerfully dedicated to my six living grandchildren (and one who is in heaven.) That they might grow up in a world in which Christians truly demonstrate a compassionate spirit of Jude 22 toward the fallen.

DOUBLE-SOUL

Table of Contents

Preface

I was lost! I had been kidnapped in a foreign country! Furthermore, I had no idea where my captors were taking me. They suddenly stopped on a dark side street. Was this *it?* No, instead they took the little money that I had in my wallet and just drove away. I was left lying in the gutter, crying and wondering.

The rancid stench and disgusting filth of the gutter completely saturated my clothing. I slowly rose to my knees and, leaning against a car, finally pulled myself out of that awful place. Drenched in my own sweat and the filth of the street, I reviewed my whole life. Why didn't they just kill me? My head was pounding and my heart was exploding in my chest. I could barely walk as I tried to determine my location so that I could make it back to my own car.

As I inched my way along the path, absolute terror tortured my mind. My hands and legs began to shake uncontrollably. I wondered if my captors would come back for me. Would they throw me in the river? Would they beat me? Would they knife me? At that moment, death seemed to be a very real possibility.

Sensing that I was being watched, I crossed the street so that I could quickly glance behind me. Yes! A young woman was measuring her steps as she followed me. Panic gripped me, and I was afraid to go directly to my car. Now what should I do? Afraid, exhausted, and filthy, I walked for over an hour. I zigzagged along the street, retracing my steps to ensure I would not be followed to my car.

Finally, realizing that there was no place else to hide, no other place of refuge, I made my way to the car. Opening the door as quickly as my trembling hands would allow, I threw myself behind the wheel, locked the doors, started the engine, and drove out of the center of the city. I had an eerie feeling that I'd been here before, but when?

As the scene of that living nightmare faded in the rearview mirror, a question gripped me. "How did I get here?" I asked, realizing how vulnerable I had been. I wept, trembled, and considered the danger to which I had exposed myself. What force drove me to this awful place?

I felt a great sense of despair as I admitted, "I need help, but who can help me? Would anyone even want to help me?"

Again I asked, "How did I get here?" Was this some terrorist or criminal abduction? No, tourists are warned of those risks. Rather, it all started with a drive ... and a wrong turn, when I made the wrong choice! Life is filled with choices for us all. Some are relatively inconsequential, some are life changing, and some are *deadly!*

CHAPTER 1

A Preacher

That which is beautiful and alluring on the surface may be downright deadly - a Venus fly trap. Such is the "Blue" Danube which divides the historical cities of Buda and Pest, making Budapest one of the most beautiful cities in Europe. Budapest is an architectural paradise with a blend of Budapest's Roman amphitheaters and ancient Gothic Cathedrals, all blended with the modern. The rising hills, the catacombs, the Parliament Building, Fisherman's Bastion, St. Stephen's Basilica, and the Buda Castle were all my favorites.

I enjoyed giving my guests tours of this beautiful city, the capital of Hungary, and one of the larger cities in the European Union. Budapest began as a Celtic settlement and became the Roman capital of Pannonia. Hungarians arrived in the territory in the 9th century. Their first settlement was pillaged by the Mongols in 1241–1242. The re-established town became one of the centers of Renaissance humanist culture in the 15th century. Following nearly 150 years of Ottoman rule, the region entered a new age of prosperity in the 18th and 19th centuries, and Budapest became a global city after the 1873 unification. It also became the second capital of the Austro-Hungarian Empire, a great power that dissolved in 1918, following World War I. Budapest was the focal point of the Hungarian Revolution of 1848, the Hungarian Republic of Councils of 1919, Operation Panzerfaust in 1944, the Battle of Budapest in 1945, and the Revolution of 1956.

Yes, Budapest *was* a beautiful city with an illustrious history. However, when darkness fell, the array of colorful lights hid the danger that existed on almost every street. Even on the famous Vaci Ut, every tourist had to guard his wallet, beware of scams, and even be prepared to be lured into the underworld. I suppose, in this way, Budapest is like any major city in any country.

This is my story. The story of a preacher, (that's right - a PREACHER), who found himself in the dark underside of a beautiful city.

As I stopped at the traffic light, my mind was tormented by a raging, internal debate. This was a question with which I had wrestled more times than I cared to admit. "Which way am I going to turn?" I knew that to turn left would mean peace and safety. I would be home. There was really no other choice to make. Why then the hesitation? Why such debate? Home is where I know that I should flee. Yet the enticement of the city and the cry of my own flesh were mesmerizing. As I contemplated the unknown that awaited me, a blaring horn interrupted my deliberation, and without another thought, I chose *the city!*

Proverbs 7

*My son, **keep my words,** and lay up my commandments with thee.*

***Keep my commandments,** and live; and my law as the apple of thine eye.*

*Bind them upon thy fingers, **write them upon the table of thine heart.***

Say unto wisdom, Thou art my sister; and call understanding thy kinswoman:

That they may keep thee from the strange woman, from the stranger which flattereth with her words.

For at the window of my house I looked through my casement,

*And beheld among the simple ones, I discerned among the youths, **a young man void of understanding,***

Passing through the street near her corner; and he went the way to her house,

In the twilight, in the evening, in the black and dark night:

And, behold, there met him a woman with the attire of an harlot, and subtle of heart.

(She is loud and stubborn; her feet abide not in her house:

Now is she without, now in the streets, and lieth in wait at every corner.)

So she caught him, and kissed him, and with an impudent face said unto him,

I have peace offerings with me; this day have I payed my vows.

Therefore came I forth to meet thee, diligently to seek thy face, and I have found thee.

I have decked my bed with coverings of tapestry, with carved works, with fine linen of Egypt.

I have perfumed my bed with myrrh, aloes, and cinnamon.

Come, let us take our fill of love until the morning: let us solace ourselves with loves.

For the good man is not at home, he is gone a long journey:

He hath taken a bag of money with him, and will come home at the day appointed.

With her much fair speech she caused him to yield, with the flattering of her lips she forced him.

He goeth after her straightway, as an ox goeth to the slaughter, or as a fool to the correction of the stocks;

Till a dart strike through his liver; as a bird hasteth to the snare, and knoweth not that it is for his life.

Hearken unto me now therefore, O ye children, and attend to the words of my mouth.

Let not thine heart decline to her ways, go not astray in her paths.

For she hath cast down many wounded: yea, many strong men have been slain by her.

Her house is the way to hell, going down to the chambers of death.

No sooner than I had pointed my car toward the city did my heart begin pounding. I knew I had made the wrong decision. Why?

There was no one in the car with me, no voices, and yet some invisible force seemed to draw me onward. I realized as I continued driving that fear, apprehension, and uncertainty were replaced with a carnal sense of expectation. I knew that my flesh, sinful and dark, was now in control. I was in the grip of something evil and overpowering.

I was familiar with the city. I had previously taken many individuals to the airport which had afforded me the opportunity to "take in the sights." I began to dwell upon various places I could visit. I could simply walk down Vaci Ut and find any number of women who would love to spend some time with me. It was a pleasant evening, so I decided to search for a parking place and then spend some time walking around. Finding a safe parking spot would not be easy. I searched for nearly an hour, and when I was about to give up and go home, I saw a car pulling out. I did not then realize how often I had been given an opportunity to abandon my foolish quest. I parked the car.

As I began walking, a chill ran through my body. I thought, "What am I doing? Where am going?" I really did not have a specific plan. I was just going to walk and see where I ended up. I dismissed the chill and the questions, though I did sense that something was *different*.

The city was alive with music, lights, and laughter. I enjoyed watching people. I amused myself as I walked block after block with no destination in mind. I had experienced this previously. One such walk found me outside an oriental massage studio. Perhaps I should visit there again tonight? I saw a young woman moving slowly toward me. She was dressed like a prostitute and smiled as she approached. I made an impotent attempt to pass her, but when she reached out and touched my arm, I knew I would not walk away.

She was distributing literature for a club, the type of club I had never visited. It was a dance club with women who had only one desire: to satisfy the flesh. She was quite friendly and volunteered to walk me to the club, which advertised tonight as a special night, featuring "free" entrance and the drink of your choice. I was not interested in any drink, but the attraction of the club was very powerful. As I allowed the young woman to lead me down the street, once again a chill ran through my body. More questions bombarded my mind. "Where am I going? Why am I going?" I thought of my wife, my children, and the ministry. I had no answers. Everything I knew told me that I should stop, turn around, and run away. "This young woman is *not* my friend!" Like an animal being led to the slaughter, I walked ever closer to the executioner.

The inner debate stopped as we approached a building and a doorman stepped forward to open the door. He mumbled something in a language I could not understand and handed the young woman some money. She said, "He will take you from here."

Without question, I followed the man. Down, down we walked into deep darkness. At the bottom of the stairs, a blinding light shone into my eyes. A rough voice demanded, "Identification papers!" I searched my pockets for my passport. Impatiently, the rough voice screamed, "Give me that," as two very large hands engulfed my shaking hands and tore away my passport. "Enter."

I thought of the times I had witnessed the slaying of a pig. No matter how much the pig squealed or tried to free itself, the sharp knife always found its mark. Now I felt like the pig, and the knife awaited on the other side of the door.

Slowly, I entered a room and another world. Several flashing lights pierced the darkness. The loud music made it almost impossible to hear. It was much cooler there than it was outside. My mouth was simultaneously wet and dry. I scanned the room filled with a dozen women all dressed for trouble. A young woman approached me and offered me a drink. I shook my head "no."

Then, without warning, there was a woman on each of my arms, taking me to a table. "Buy us a drink. Sit. Let's talk. You want to dance?" Immediately, I said, "No, no, no." I knew that I needed to leave, but the drinks came anyway. The young ladies tried to persuade me to take them to another room. Again, I exclaimed, "No, no, no!" I got up and tried to leave when an imposing figure of a man came to the table and asked, "Is there a problem? Sit down. Do you not enjoy the ladies?"

Now I knew that I was in real - very real - danger. How could I be so stupid? I wondered, "What is going to happen to me?"

I said, "I have made a horrible mistake. I need to leave." The man just stood blocking my path until one of the women motioned to let me passs. Stepping aside, the man grabbed my arm and said, "You pay your bill over here," as he pushed me toward a dimly lit bar.

An older lady behind the bar scribbled some figures on a dirty piece of paper and handed it to me. I took out what I thought was the correct amount and handed it to the older lady. She said something to another man standing at the bar. Speaking in English that was barely understandable, he told me I did not have enough money. I was sure there was some mistake. I had given the lady the equivalent of thirty dollars. As I tried to explain, two extremely large men suddenly pulled back my arms and took away my wallet. They began taking out papers, money, and credit cards. A third man with a flashlight began carefully reading each card.

I said, "I don't understand. I have paid you."

The man with the flashlight scoffed, "Thirty dollars? You think you have paid us. You owe us THREE HUNDRED DOLLARS! You have given us nothing."

Three hundred dollars? I could not believe it. How could I have been so careless? What was I doing here? I did not have three hundred dollars. The United States Embassy consistently issued warnings about such establishments which pilfered unwary foreigners. Yes, I was a foreigner, but more than that I was a preacher!

A conference was being conducted in front of me. They were not happy. The older lady kept asking, "Are you sure you do not have more money?" One of the younger women came over from the table. Putting her arm around me, she whispered in my ear, "Please give them what they want. I will help you. I will go with you to the back room."

"You do not understand. I do not have any money." I tried in vain to convince them that I had nothing and was only on my way home. Perspiring profusely, my head pounding and my chest tightening, I nearly passed out. They sat me down and gave me a glass of water. It was at this point that I realized that there was nothing that I could do.

"Take him out of here," screamed the man with the flashlight.

The two strong men dragged me up the long flight of stairs. The young woman from the table said, "Wait! I am going to go with you."

"Where am I going?" I wondered. "What are they going to do to me?"

There was no doubt in my mind that this was going to be the night that I would die. I had disobeyed, and had chosen my flesh one too many times. Surely, God's patience had run out.

As we reached the top of the stairs, an SUV drove up and stopped in front of the door. The young woman from the table opened the back door and I was thrown in, falling down to the floor. The young woman helped me up, and one of the strong men got in beside me. I had no idea where I was being taken. All the while, the young woman kept saying, "Pay them, and they won't hurt you. Give them what they want." She kept her arm around me and laid her head on my shoulder.

I kept repeating, "I do not have any money. I do not have any money. I just want to go home. I just want to go home." Right, but *why* did I want to go home? Was it love of God? Was it obedience to Him? Or was it, "Lord, just get me out of this mess!"

I had no idea how long I had been at the club. I did not know where I was, nor how long they had been driving.

Suddenly, the SUV stopped. As I looked out the window, I could see the Danube. I could smell the water. "Is this where they are going to kill me?" It was quiet with very few people on the street. If they wanted to kill me, there would be few, if any, witnesses.

The noise of the door opening interrupted my thoughts, and I was pulled out of the SUV and thrown to the ground. "Get up," screamed the driver whom I now recognized as the man who had been holding the flashlight at the club. The two strong men lifted me off the ground and dragged me toward the river. I tried in vain to pull away. The men knew their job. "No," ordered the driver. "Bring him over here."

"Over where?" I wondered. I looked up and saw a glassed in enclosure with bright lights. A lady peered out at us as the driver took my wallet from my jacket and said, "Here, get us the money, now!"

I fumbled through my wallet for a credit card. As I pulled out one credit card, I cast a pleading glance toward the lady behind the glass, hoping for her help. She only asked, "How much money do you want?" I slipped the card into the drawer beneath the window.

"How much do I want?" I thought to myself? "Nothing. I don't want anything. I don't have any money. I want to go home."

The lady returned and announced, "Declined."

The driver then took out card after card, but each time the answer was the same. "Declined!"

Exasperated and angry, they dragged me back to the SUV. The young woman linked her arm around mine and said, "It is going to be okay. Don't worry." I didn't believe her. I felt no comfort whatsoever.

We started driving along the river. The lights dimmed behind us. Just then a phone rang. Following a short conversation, we veered away from the Danube and started toward the center of the city.

Now, I had absolutely no idea what their game was nor where they were taking me. Then they stopped on a dark side street. Was this where I would die? They took my money and drove away. I was left lying in the gutter, and I felt as filthy as that gutter.

As I navigated the five hour drive home, I had to stop several times to vomit. I was physically, emotionally, and spiritually depleted. "This is not who I really am nor the life I wanted to live." The moment I entered the club, I knew I did not belong there. I had never been to such a place before. I realized that I was not in control. Nevertheless, I had no explanation! "What drove me?"

The same questions echoed over and over in my mind and heart. "Why? Why? Why? What is wrong with me? How can I do this?" For over twenty-seven years I had wrestled with these questions. Deep down, I knew how close I had come to being killed, and for what - for a few moments of false pleasure?

"How long," I wondered, "would a holy God allow me to act so foolishly, and so selfishly and yet not discipline me?" I knew that *whatsoever a man soweth, that shall he also reap.*

Like many men, I struggled with the lust of the flesh, the lust of the eyes, and the pride of life, but unlike other men, for twenty-seven years I had lived a double-life, as a hypocrite and a phony. I was a sexual addict! I was trying to serve God, but I was periodically binging in graphic sin. I was dying.

How do I know this? I know this because I experienced the indescribable pain! I felt a complete loss of hope. I was overwhelmed by a sense of fear and guilt. "What if my wife, church members, or Christian leaders really knew of my sin? Would they no longer care for me? I was haunted by the thought that the standard treatment in Bible-believing circles is that they simply shoot their own wounded. Once I was discovered, my fears proved to be well-founded. I was all but abandoned by most of my co-workers, family, and friends.

Yes, I had served as a pastor, a Christian educator, and a missionary. I want you to understand as you continue reading this book that in no way do I wish to magnify myself, my sin, nor all that I have now lost because of my sin. It is my desire to warn you that Satan desires to entrap you and then expose you in order to destroy your family, ruin your testimony, and bring shame upon the name of our holy God. I want you to comprehend that what you whisper in private will be shouted in public. I am writing to thousands of laymen, pastors, missionaries, and evangelists who wrestle with sins of the flesh, perhaps in secret.

On my own, I would never have chosen to share my story with you. I cannot begin to count the number of times that I wanted to quit. Many times I begged the Lord to raise up someone else to stand in the gap. He did not give me liberty to be silent! The Lord revealed to me that I was a waverer, a double-souled man. If I were really going to have victory, I needed to stand in the gap. And so this is my story, written because a majority of Bible believers will be tempted in the next 24 hours, and some will make a deadly choice. Remember, just like the underside of Budapest, what appears to be beautiful and alluring, may be deadly.

James 1:13 - 15
Let no man say when he is tempted, I am tempted of God: for

God cannot be tempted with evil, neither tempteth he any man: But every man is tempted, when he is drawn away of his own lust, and enticed. Then when lust hath conceived, it bringeth forth sin: and sin, when it is finished, bringeth forth death.

Conversations with Brother Gabe

Dr. Brad Weniger: You were very near death, weren't you?

Brother Gabriel Rivera: Yes, I was. If my addiction didn't kill me, those men were ready to do the job. You never truly believe the worst will happen, but it nearly did. Galatians 6:7, 8, *"Be not deceived; God is not mocked: for whatsoever a man soweth, that shall he also reap. For he that soweth to his flesh shall of the flesh reap corruption; but he that soweth to the Spirit shall of the Spirit reap life everlasting."*

Dr. Brad Weniger: Looking back, what steps might have been taken to prevent this episode from ever occurring?

Brother Gabriel Rivera: The Bible tells us that it's not good for the man to be alone. I would have given *anything* if my wife (or a male co-worker) would have gone with me, but that was rarely the case. Accountability is everything when one has an addiction or a serious preoccupation with sin. Here are my recommendations to *anyone* when they travel. 1. Travel with someone. 2. Call before, during, and after travel. 3. Turn off electronics including the television. 4. Read your Bible. 5. Don't go out.

Dr. Brad Weniger: Those are great guidelines for travel! On another subject you used the term "double-souled." Where did you first run across that term, and were you "double-souled"?

Brother Gabriel Rivera: James 1:8 says, "A double-minded man is unstable in all his ways." The phrase "double-minded" grabbed my attention. This verse described *me!* The Jamiesson – Faussett – Brown Commentary on James uses the word "double-souled." The sense here is that one soul is directed toward God, the other toward something else.

Dr. Brad Weniger: Would you say that an unrepentant sexual addict is potentially in a constant state of "double-soul-ness" then?

Brother Gabriel Rivera: Yes, absolutely. The sex addict, as Adam Clarke's commentary states it, has two souls: one for earth and one for heaven. He wants heaven, but he cannot let earth go. Until the sex addict can admit that he has sinned against God, he will never be able to repent.

Dr. Brad Weniger: It's true that you were "driven" to these episodes. While you *were* responsible for your behavior, how strong were your compulsions? Were they physical? Mental? Spiritual?

Brother Gabriel Rivera: No one believes that one day they'll become an addict. The addict takes that first step innocently seeking to satisfy his flesh. Whether you call it lust, compulsion, or a craving, the truth is that the sex addict truly believes he is in control. The reality is, the addict has become enslaved. It is a voluntary act of foolishness. My cravings were physical, mental, and spiritual. I had to act out so that my flesh would be satisfied. Mentally, I did not consider the consequences. Spiritually, I convinced myself that I had no choice.

Dr. Brad Weniger: Finally, how *can* a born-again Christian commit such sin? Let me state it this way: Does the Bible address the question of a Christian's graphic sins?

Brother Gabriel Rivera: I John 1:9 says, *"If we confess our sins, he is faithful and just to forgive us our sins, and to cleanse us from all unrighteousness."* Matthew Henry, the well-known Bible expositor, once said, *"Though God may suffer his people to fall into sin, he will not suffer his people to lie still in it."* God will never abandon his children. You may be a Christian but have become sloppy in your relationship to God. You believe God will somehow take care of you and work everything out, even if you do as you please. You flirt with sin and think that you can get away with it. God's love demands fatherly chastisement. If you do not repent, God will send judgment. God will break your life into little pieces until you learn what kind of God you are dealing with, and you come to appreciate the One Who has called you to be His own.

Dr. Brad Weniger: AMEN. That's *real* food for thought!

Brother Gabriel Rivera: *Soul* food.

Dr. Brad Weniger: Right! *Soul* food. Ha! That's good!

DOUBLE-SOUL

CHAPTER 2

The Balaam Strategy

... the doctrine of Balaam, who taught Balac to cast a stumbling block before the children of Israel ... and to commit fornication.

Revelation 2:14

We can find ourselves in the pages of the Bible, God's Word. The book of Numbers, chapters 22 through 25, records for us the account of Balaam and Balak. Balaam possessed some knowledge of the true God, and he believed that his superior powers as poet and prophet were derived from God. His fame was great, and he became **conceited** and **covetous**. (We will deal with these later.)

Balak, the king of Moab, entered into a league with the Midianites against Israel and sent emissaries to Balaam asking him to come and "curse" Israel, because Israel was too strong for him. The emissaries arrived "with the fees for his services in their hand". Balaam must have had some misgivings about their intentions, because he asked them to stay overnight while he waited upon the Lord. In this, Balaam showed some wisdom in wanting to know the mind of the Lord. God told Balaam not to go with them and not to curse Israel (Numbers 22:12). Having received an answer from the Lord, at first Balaam refused to go with the messengers, and they returned to Balak.

However, here is a point worth noting: Satan is never easily deterred in his endeavor to derail God's plan or people. He is patient, and he claims that he is "right". Like the Devil, Balak refused to take "no" for an answer. Balak's response was to send a larger party of more honorable princes - with the promise of a much greater reward. This time, the Lord gave Balaam permission to go on one condition: "If the men come to call you" (Numbers 22:20).

Balaam replied that he could not be tempted by reward, but that he would speak what God should reveal. He requested that they remain for the night in order that he might know what the Lord would say to him concerning the matter. However, note that Balaam did not wait for the men to call to him, but rather arose and prepared to go with them. God became angry with Balaam.

Why? Because he disobeyed God's instructions. God had told Balaam if the messengers came to call him, then he could go with them. Instead, Balaam exercised his own will. Willfulness is an open door for Satan.

It is here that "great men", "the famous", or "the well-known men" often fall prey to the Balaam strategy. Such men are greatly tempted because they are specifically targeted. This comes in waves of temptation and testing in a satanic effort to "overwhelm" us. *"Deep calleth unto deep at the noise of thy waterspouts: all thy waves and thy billows are gone over me"* Psalm 42:7.

What is the Balaam Strategy? The answer is clear. Balaam had become conceited. He understood something that we fail to understand: if the enemy can discover what it is that we desire more than we desire to obey God, we can be defeated by seduction. The marvelous spiritual gifts that he possessed, Balaam willingly prostituted. He was intoxicated with his own position and power. More than likely, he was flattered, too, by the attention he received from King Balak and his princes. All these evil lusts, money, power, and position, grow out of the same soil: **PRIDE**.

Had Balaam lived among today's evangelicals, he would have been considered a great man. His public sayings would be widely known, and his "ministry" would have great impact (Numbers 22:6). In his day, Balaam was also known for his "prayer power." That is, when he spoke to the Lord, Balaam usually got an answer (Numbers

22:8, 18). He certainly would have felt right at home among many of today's televangelists.

Balaam was known for getting answers from God, but, caught up with his own notoriety, he pursued a course of action with Balak which God deemed reckless. It took divine intervention to get Balaam to wake up and stop a course of action that would dishonor God and God's people, and would position Balaam at risk of mortal danger. Balaam, blinded by his own desires, was rescued by a donkey who knew enough to take God at His Word!

God's Word is clear. God's instructions for a particular matter have been stated. Yet, we think we have to do it our way. We would never say that we know more than God, but our actions expose our true theology.

One of the most effective methods of the enemy of our soul is the Balaam Strategy. It is an attack upon every man's character that is invisible to the naked eye. It is a spiritual assault upon your walk and relationship with Jesus Christ. It does not have the power to curse you, but is very capable of corrupting you.

Today Satan is looking for a motive or desire that will remove you from your God ordained responsibility and purpose. My friend, that means whether you are the pastor, the missionary, the Christian school teacher, the Bible College professor, the deacon, the worship leader, or if you are the pillar of the community and church, you are in danger.

Unless you are walking in the Spirit daily, you will fall. I know, I know. You do not believe that it could ever happen *to you*. Well, Satan has you right where he wants you! Remember, "Pride *goeth* before destruction, and an haughty spirit before a fall," Proverbs 16:18. He has you believing a lie, the lie that says, "It won't happen to me." In essence, you are denying your humanity.

Balaam desired to help Balak destroy the Israelites. When he arrived in Moab, and viewed Israel, he could not curse what God had blessed. Balaam tried three times, but each time Israel was blessed. "How shall I curse, whom God hath not cursed? Or how shall I defy, *whom* the LORD hath not defied?" (Numbers 23:10)

Balak had paid Balaam well to curse Israel, yet without success. Balak was very angry that Israel had been blessed, rather than cursed. However, Balaam found "Plan B" to appease the King and earn his money. Balaam gave counsel to Balak on what to do to get God angry at Israel. If he could not *curse* Israel he would *corrupt* Israel. Balaam proposed a different strategy against them (Numbers 31:16). Balaam taught Balak to corrupt the people who could not be cursed (Numbers 31:15-16; 22:5-6; 23:8) by seducing them to marry Moabite women and thereby commit spiritual adultery (James 4:4).

If the Moabite women could entice the Israelites into idolatry and immorality, it would not be necessary to curse them. God Himself would bring judgment upon them. Balaam's "Plan B" succeeded, and 24,000 Israelites perished under God's judgment (Numbers 25:1–9).

Think about this for a moment with me. Balaam was *a prophet*. He had a knowledge of God and had supernatural gifts from God. However, when we look at the total man, what do we see? A man who was conceited, covetous, and corrupt.

Receiving a spiritual gift does not change a person's character. Let that sink in! If a person were proud, unreliable, or deceitful before receiving a spiritual gift, that person will *still be* proud or unreliable or deceitful after receiving it.

However, receiving such a gift does increase a person's responsibility, because it increases the influence he can have on others. It also presents the temptation to view our Christian life in terms of spiritual gifts in place of building godly character. We will all leave this earth one day. Only our character will remain.

Of course, this is not merely Balaam's strategy. It is Satan's strategy, and he has employed it throughout history. Do you really believe that you are a match for the devil? Consider the following examples.

Samson's birth was foretold by an angel. He would be a Nazarite, separated unto the Lord. He drank no wine nor cut his hair as marks of his vow. Nevertheless, he saw a Philistine woman to whom he was attracted. He sought her against his parents' wishes. His involvement with her created a conflict with the Philistines.

Samson was anointed, powerful, and feared. At one point, he killed a thousand of the enemy.

Then Samson met Delilah. She managed to get Samson to reveal his secret to her. No razor had ever touched his long hair which symbolized his covenant with God and his purpose for living. Delilah betrayed Samson. He was captured, blinded, and put to hard labor grinding grain. After a while, his hair grew back. I have often wondered, "How long did it take for Samson's hair to grow back?" The pain and the shame that was Samson's was because of what he SAW. When he was brought for sport into the temple of Dagon, he pulled down the pillars, killing himself and three thousand Philistines. He is numbered among the heroes of faith in Hebrews 11, but he went through an awful ordeal, because he lost SIGHT of his mission.

We all know the story of David, the anointed shepherd-king of Israel.

David, killed a lion, a bear, and a giant! He expanded the territory of Israel and prepared for the temple, but he lost sight of his purpose and set his eyes on Bathsheba. Then, he sent her husband to the front lines of battle where he was killed.

Do you see the pattern? What the Moabites could not do to Israel, what the Philistines could not do to Samson, and what the enemies could not do to David, they all did to themselves! Friend, this will happen to you if you are not aware of the Balaam Strategy. If Satan can discover what we want more than we want God's will, he will offer it. He will offer anything to get us away from God: sex, money, or power.

That Balaam had a clear understanding concerning the death of the righteous is evident from Numbers 23:10, "Who can count the dust of Jacob, and the number of the fourth *part* of Israel? Let me die the death of the righteous, and let my last end be like his!"

His prayer was not answered. He was executed in God's judgment upon the Moabites, whose money had tempted him to align himself against God.

When considering the knowledge that Balaam possessed, and the revelations he had received, one can only conclude that he got exactly what he deserved. His conduct had been exceedingly sinful.

My friend, you too will receive exactly what you deserve. As you continue reading my story, I want you to know that I am *not* "a victim." I am responsible for my sin. I did not recognize Balaam's Strategy. I believed that I merely had a besetting sin. I deceived myself. In so doing, I lost everyone whom I loved and cherished. It is only by the Grace and Mercy of God that I am alive to share with you the truths that had to be written on my heart through experiences of pain, suffering, and shame. You do *not* want to walk in my steps! There is no substitute for obeying God.

Conversations with Brother Gabe

Dr. Brad Weniger: WOW! That Balaam strategy is a real eye opener! I believe the single sentence which grabbed my attention in that last chapter was "receiving a spiritual gift does not change a person's character."

Brother Gabriel Rivera: I would be glad to. I lived a double-life for twenty-seven years. I struggled with sexual sin, every two or three years giving into the lust of my flesh. I used anger to control people. Yet, I was what most people considered a gifted individual. I was experiencing blessings and leading a fruitful ministry. The gifts that were natural and those that were God-given did not change me. Why? I failed to draw close to Christ.

Dr. Brad Weniger: You go on to talk about "increased responsibility." Is it possible that some long-time Christians are self-deceived in thinking that they've really mastered Christianity 101, 201, 301, 401, (and so on,) to such a degree that character-development isn't a major priority? Do they "fake it 'till they make it", so to speak?

Brother Gabriel Rivera: I think that is definitely true. Matthew 7:22, 23 says, *"Many will say to me in that day, Lord, Lord, have we not prophesied in thy name? And in thy name have we cast out devils? And in thy name done many wonderful works? And then will I profess unto them, I never knew you: depart from me, ye that work iniquity."* These verses terrified me. I could not reconcile my actions and my character with what I knew God's Word taught.

Since I was a "binger" seeking to satisfy my flesh every two or three years, I convinced myself that I had a "besetting" sin. Though I was being given more responsibilities, I knew that I was guilty of compromising character. Even my character was double-souled.

Dr. Brad Weniger: My! That means some long time Christians are "easy pickins" for the Devil on a daily basis. Would you agree that they are sort of the Devil's *plaything?*

Brother Gabriel Rivera: Yes, I am afraid you are correct. The Devil has always targeted those in position of leadership. That is not a secret. It is imperative that men, such as you and I, stay intimate in our relationship with Jesus Christ. Our first responsibility is to be in a right relationship with Christ. We are often so busy doing the work of the ministry that we fall into the trap of just getting by on our natural gifts.

Dr. Brad Weniger: You say you're "not a victim." I assume that you mean you had *a choice* to do right, and that God provided *the means* to do right, but you willfully and deliberately "caved in" when tempted? Is that right?

Brother Gabriel Rivera: You are correct. I want to be very clear when I say, 'I am not a victim." I Corinthians 10:13 is clear, *"There hath no temptation taken you but such as is common to man: but God is faithful, who will not suffer you to be tempted above that ye are able; but will with the temptation also make a way to escape, that ye may be able to bear it."* To say that I was a victim, would be to make God a liar. This is not easy for me. While I gave the outward appearance of being a gifted, strong leader and communicator, I was not. I had to work very hard. I had a tough exterior, because I was not strong in the Lord, and that was my fault. God gave me every opportunity to grow in Him and to flee temptation. I was undisciplined. I did not know how to say "NO!"

Dr. Brad Weniger: If you could, would you like to go back and do things differently?

Brother Gabriel Rivera: Absolutely! Without hesitation! If only I would have allowed the Lord to have all of me. There are so many things I would do differently.

Dr. Brad Weniger: Was *any* of that sin *worth it?*

Brother Gabriel Rivera: No. I was so foolish. Sin - my sin - cost me my family and my ministry. I hurt so many people.

Dr. Brad Weniger: Those of you who are contemplating sin, listen to Brother Gabe. "There is no substitute for obeying God."

CHAPTER 3

Double Minded Men

Let's return to that horrible night in Budapest. I could have been killed! And yet, as I drove back to Romania that night, I gave careful consideration to completing that very job that the Hungarians had left undone. Suicide? Yes, you see, I had no desire to live. I had broken my marriage vows, and I had betrayed my Lord and those who were supporting our ministry. My mind, my emotions, and my spirit were all attempting to communicate with me at the same time. I screamed out in despair, "Leave me alone!"

Thank God, His Word never leaves us, and The Devil, who knows this, has access to our very thoughts. James 1:8, "A double-minded man *is* unstable in all his ways," played over and over in my head. Louder and louder. Taunting me, laughing at me. I had conversations with myself. "Who could I talk to? Where can I get help? Why am I so drawn to sexual sin? What if someone catches me?" I had no reasonable answers for the questions that pierced my soul. I felt like an addict. A hopeless repeat-offender. Little did I realize …

This was not the first time that I was confronted with these questions. I did not find myself in the gutter in Budapest overnight. It took twenty-seven years of disobedience. Oh, how far I had fallen!

I understood that double-minded literally means "double-souled," with one soul directed toward God, and the other toward *something else*. It was that *something else,* every two or three years, that drove me to such a Budapest experience.

The words in James 1:7, "For let not **that man** ("double-souled") think that he shall receive any thing of the Lord," seemed clear. As long as I am unstable, I will not, I cannot, receive anything from the Lord.

Although my sinful activities would occur intermittently (that is, I would go years without failure), I was never free. Moral failure was followed by confession, guilt, remorse, anger, physical illness, and a renewed commitment to never do it again! Of course, I would fail again and again and again. I really thought that I could control my sin. But the truth was that I was being controlled by my sin. I seemed to take comfort in that it was *only* every two or three years. I was suffering from "double-soul-ness".

There was the occasion on which I confessed my sin of viewing internet pornography to my wife. Our relationship became estranged following my confession, and I knew that it was my fault. I knew that I was a double-minded man. Upon my confession, we sought counsel. For one week, we went to a Biblical counselor. Unfortunately, out of fear and for other reasons, I confessed only my involvement with internet pornography. Nothing else.

The result of this partial confession was that I experienced a five year reprieve. I was ecstatic! Little did I know that soon I was to fail once more. This failure would take me deeper into sin. This time was different. I was terrified. I had gone to counseling and had experienced five years of moral reprieve. Despair flooded my soul. I had moved beyond internet pornography. "How? Why? What am I going to do?" The normal excuses and resolutions seemed hollow. I was afraid and alone. My past arguments of self-justification: "I have a besetting sin," "it is a spiritual attack," "I will never do this again," all seemed to mock me.

You see, I did not know that I was a double-souled man. Double-soul-ness is not something that Satan wants you to recognize. I had succumbed to the Balaam Strategy. I was a preacher. I had helped other people face *their* sins. At one point I even thought that it was God's fault. "Why doesn't He deliver me from this sin?" I even begged the Lord to take me out of this life. I confessed that He could not trust me here on earth any longer. "For your sake - and for your glory, please, just take me home." He did not!

I am the oldest of five children. My mother and father divorced when I was six years old. Up to that time, we had been reared to be Seventh Day Adventists. My mother was awarded custody of all five children. Following the divorce, my mother began searching, and we visited several churches. We began attending a Baptist church, because at one time my mother had attended a Baptist church. In fact, she was saved in an old German Baptist church, but, because of her marriage to my father, a Puerto Rican, she was not made to feel welcome there any longer.

When we began attending the church, I enjoyed it, and I knew a lot of the young people from school. They had a basketball league which I also enjoyed. The Bible stories seemed to be the same as they were at the Adventist church. I won memorizing contests, invited people to Sunday school, and thoroughly enjoyed myself. However, I was not *saved*.

During the summer of 1967, I was with my father on vacation in his hometown. During the day, I was ill, and, that night I had trouble sleeping. Lying there in bed, I was overwhelmed with a feeling of loss. I had this image of my mother becoming ill and dying. Since I was the oldest, I had become my mother's best friend. I became a father figure to my brothers and sisters.

As I lay there crying, wondering about my mother, Bible verses which I had memorized came to mind. Verses about Christ, the cross, and the stories about the disciples all flooded my mind. As I beheld Calvary, I could see Mary, John and Christ. I could see the disciples, feel their sadness, and experience their wonder. What would they do now that Jesus was gone? As I considered all of these things, I thought about my mother. If she were gone, what would she want me to do? She would want me to take care of my brothers and sisters, get a good education, and live for God. Live for God? It was then that it hit me.

How could I live for God? I did not know Him! What if the disciples had walked away in sadness and shame? What if they had not believed on Him? We would have no gospel. I then realized why Christ came. He came to die for me. He came that I might have life.

Right there, alone in that bedroom in Puerto Rico, I asked Christ to save me. I knew that I was a sinner and that I had never applied Calvary to me. I told Him that I loved Him, and that I wanted to live for Him. I received Jesus Christ as my Personal Savior when I was thirteen years of age in July, 1967, in Fajardo, Puerto Rico.

My second prayer of faith that night was to tell the Lord that I did not know if my mother were alive or dead, but that I would trust Him. I would take care of my brothers and sisters, get an education, and I would live for Him.

One week later, when we got back to Patterson, New Jersey, I called home. I waited anxiously for an answer. The voice I heard was the voice of my mother! I immediately told her that I was saved. It would be a couple more days before we would be home in Iowa, and I would have the opportunity to let the pastor know that I was saved. They wanted me to be baptized right away. However, I had always struggled with understanding God's Grace. Even then, I felt like I needed to change so that people could see the change, know that I was saved, and then I would be baptized. My pastor explained to me that God will do the changing, and that I needed only to be obedient. So I was obedient, and I was baptized.

At the age of fifteen, while I was at a Youth Retreat weekend, I dedicated my life to serve the Lord full-time. During the invitation at the closing service, the preacher asked everyone to bow their heads and close their eyes. One hundred and twenty five youth were asked, "If you would like to give your life to Christ for full-time Christian service, I want you to stand up and look at me." I knew that God was speaking to me. I knew that I wanted to serve Him with my life. So, I stood up and looked at him. When I did, I saw that I was the only person to stand! Right then and there, God clearly demonstrated to me that He had called me to His ministry.

I became a leader in my youth group. I visited nursing homes. I went to camp every summer. Under the mentorship of my pastor, I had the opportunity to preach my first sermon when I was seventeen years old. I went to summer school for three weeks at the Moody Bible Institute. I loved the Lord, His work, and His people.

I left home to attend Bible school in Michigan, and later transferred to a school in Iowa, where I met my wife to be. I pastored for a total eleven years in Missouri and Pennsylvania. For the next twenty-one years, I was the director of a Mission.

However, I was a double-minded man. Remember James 1:7, 8? "For let not that man think that he shall receive any thing of the Lord. A double-minded man is unstable in all his ways." I was not just a hypocrite, but a "fickle," "wavering" man.

I convinced those around me that I was a mature, decisive, genuine leader who could get things done. However, these are external traits. Inwardly, I struggled with confidence, and was too scared to let anyone see it. After all, I had always been told that I was going be greatly used of God and that I was a gifted preacher. My mother appointed me the leader of a home, broken by divorce and sexual sin. I was constantly told, "People will follow you, and there is nothing that you cannot accomplish."

When I was three or four years old, my grandfather passed away. A picture was taken of me, standing by my grandmother, holding her hand. The story that accompanied that picture was that I was comforting my grandmother. I looked up to her and said, "It's all right Grandmother. You have me."

When I was six, my father and mother came home from the hospital with my new baby brother. My father threw my baby brother on the sofa and said, "There, you have your baby. Now I want a divorce." When my baby brother hit the sofa, he bounced so high in the air that I ran to catch him. I held him tightly as my mother wept bitter tears.

I am not certain what role these early events had in my life, nor do I offer them as excuses, for there is no excuse. I only know that I was determined to never, ever let anybody down. When I was told and retold all of these things (and more), it *became* who I was. I took on the role of leader. I accepted the responsibility for my mother, brothers, and sisters. I did the shopping for groceries and clothes, paid the bills, and, when necessary, took my siblings to the doctor. Little did I realize that, even then, my adversary, the devil, was planting seeds of destruction – seeds he would harvest at a future time and which would create the most pain and destruction possible to my family, my friends, my co-workers, and to my Savior.

It is my purpose to warn you that Satan desires to entrap you and expose you in order to ruin your testimony and bring shame upon the name of our holy God. I want to exhort you that what you whisper in private will be shouted in public. I am attempting to share with you my story because I do not want to see another husband, father, wife, mother, or child experience the pain that sexual sin will bring. I do not want to see our Lord grieved by those whom He has gifted. At all costs, I want to stand in the gap (even if I must stand alone) and let you know that Christ will never forsake you. I want you to know that there are no secrets!

Luke 8:17 says, "For nothing is secret, that shall not be made manifest; neither anything hid, that shall not be known and come abroad."

Conversations with Brother Gabe

Dr. Brad Weniger: I'm intrigued with your statement: "I was never free." You thought you "could control" your sin. Based upon your personal experience, would you say that an addict must have divine intervention to be truly "free"?

Brother Gabriel Rivera: Absolutely! We are spiritual beings. We are created with a God consciousness. The word "addiction" implies that the individual has an illness. When we view an addict as being ill, the addict's individual responsibility is removed. Romans 6:16 says, *"Know ye not, that to whom ye yield yourselves servants to obey, his servants ye are to whom ye obey; whether of sin unto death, or of obedience unto righteousness?"* When an addict, that is when I, yielded to my flesh, I was giving control to Satan. I was a slave to sin. The only person who can remove our sin is Jesus Christ. We must live in a right relationship to Jesus Christ.

Dr. Brad Weniger: Suppose an addict goes to a purely secular source for help, and that secular source does *not* acknowledge the soul of that addict. Walk me through the likely scenario of that addict's experience.

Brother Gabriel Rivera: The most popular theory of addiction is the medical model. This model views addiction as an illness with genetic or physical causes. The first step for the addicted person is to acknowledge their addiction problem. The next step is to get help. Treatment options for addiction depend on several factors, including what type of substance it is and how it affects the patients. Typically, treatment includes a combination of inpatient and outpatient programs, counseling (psychotherapy), self-help groups, pairing with individual sponsors, and medication. Apart from the power of God, the addict is powerless in changing his desires. Change begins in the heart.

Dr. Brad Weniger: You mentioned your mother, and the role she played in your life. How important are "key" family relationships in a child's early development, and how can these relationships affect a potential addiction or preoccupation with sin?

Brother Gabriel Rivera: It is very important that we never take for granted everyday interactions. I believe that these everyday interactions are more important than most parents realize. One of my favorite experiences with my mother was when she would put my brothers and sisters to bed and we would go downtown to the local Maid-Rite sandwich shop. She would buy us a Maid-Rite and we would go home to watch a movie. More importantly, my mother also shaped my theology concerning forgiveness. I was only six years old when my father divorced my mother. He left us for another "very young" woman.

Mother said, "He is your father and she (my step-mother) is your fathers wife. You don't need to love her, but you *will* respect her." My father introduced me to a world that did not respect relationships or vows. I believe that I really learned from him how to be "double-souled." By that I mean that he always lived in multiple worlds. As any other young man, I wanted to be like my father. Yet, I hated what he had done to my mother. I hated it so much that I vowed I would never be like him. I focused so much on never becoming like him that I did not know that I had unconsciously followed in his steps. No matter who we are, where we live, or what our goals may be, we all have one thing in common: a heritage.

Dr. Brad Weniger: You displayed some strong leadership qualities as a young man, but no one uncovered what was lacking in your character. Since there may be other gifted young people who are "double-souled," what do you suggest to youth workers?

Brother Gabriel Rivera: Make time to listen to your young people. Make an effort to empathize with them and to understand their world. Be careful about using your young people to make your program look successful. Make time to minister to them one on one. Make the prayer and Bible study, not the fun activities, the center of your program. I do not remember anybody asking me how I felt, or what I thought, or what I really needed. Of course, I was enjoying myself. I was the center of attention. It was easy for me to just go along. Everybody knew about our family.

Dr. Brad Weniger: You said, "Christ will *never* forsake you." There were times you must have *felt* forsaken. For the sake of your readers, is there a difference between what you may have *felt* at some point and what actually was the case? On what can a child of God rely even in trying times?

Brother Gabriel Rivera: Our relationship to Christ is not based upon how we *feel*. Our relationship is based upon the finished work of Christ on Calvary and the veracity of his Word. Now, Satan wants us to believe that we are alone. Satan wants us to doubt God's Word. Satan wants us to continue in our sin. Satan knows how we *feel*. Satan knows that our sin has pulled us away from faithfulness to Christ. We have ceased to read His Word. Our voice has become silent to Christ's ears. The only way to overcome the devil is by confessing, repenting, and turning again to the Word of God. Revelation 12:11, *"And they overcame him by the blood of the Lamb, and by the word of their testimony; and they loved not their lives unto the death."*

Dr. Brad Weniger: Can you take that to the bank of heaven?

Brother Gabriel Rivera: Absolutely. You can "take that to the bank of heaven!"

CHAPTER 4

Do You See Yourself?

Lot
Genesis 19:1 – 11

*"And there came two angels to Sodom at even; and Lot sat
in the gate of Sodom: and Lot seeing them rose up to meet them;
and he bowed himself with his face toward the ground; And he said,
Behold now, my lords, turn in, I pray you, into your servant's house,
and tarry all night, and wash your feet, and ye shall rise up early,
and go on your ways. And they said, Nay; but we will abide in the
street all night. And he pressed upon them greatly; and they turned
in unto him, and entered into his house; and he made them a feast,
and did bake unleavened bread, and they did eat.*

*But before they lay down, the men of the city, even the men
of Sodom, compassed the house round, both old and young, all the
people from every quarter: And they called unto Lot, and said unto
him, Where are the men which came in to thee this night? bring
them out unto us, that we may know them. And Lot went out at the
door unto them, and shut the door after him, And said, I pray you,
brethren, do not so wickedly.*

*Behold now, I have two daughters which have not known man;
let me, I pray you, bring them out unto you, and do ye to them as
is good in your eyes: only unto these men do nothing; for therefore
came they under the shadow of my roof. And they said, Stand back.
And they said again, This one fellow came in to sojourn, and he will*

needs be a judge: now will we deal worse with thee, than with them. And they pressed sore upon the man, even Lot, and came near to break the door. But the men put forth their hand, and pulled Lot into the house to them, and shut to the door. And they smote the men that were at the door of the house with blindness, both small and great: so that they wearied themselves to find the door."

The term *sexual addiction* is only twenty-five years old, but it describes the very real problem of extreme sexual behavior. This behavior is destructive to self and others. Experts believe tens of millions of people are addicted to sex.

Porn in the Church

- 51% of pastors say Internet pornography is a possible temptation.
- 50% of all Christian men and
- 20% of all Christian women say they are addicted to pornography.
- 75% of pastors do not make themselves accountable to anyone for their Internet use.
- Regular church attendees are 26% less likely to look at porn, however, self-identified "fundamentalists" are 91% more likely to look at porn.

Meditate upon these questions. What motivates a man? What motivates you? Why do you do the things you choose to do? Even believers can do wicked things, because of what motivates them. I know!

In the Bible, Lot chose to live among the wicked in Sodom because he loved money and prominence. However, Peter still refers to Lot as "righteous Lot." He was a double-minded man, or by my previous definition, a double-souled man - a man who allowed someone or something to come between him and his love for God. Oh, he wanted to serve God, but he also wanted to enjoy the pleasures of this world.

Today, this is exactly where many men find themselves, having a desire to serve God, but daily lured by the lust of this world. It is evident from the fact that Lot chose to live in the plain bordering the wicked cities of Sodom and Gomorrah (Genesis 13:1-13) that he was a spiritually weak man. Once he moved into the city itself and became a part of its culture, it was only a matter of time before he would drift further from God. It's true that he didn't give up his belief in the high moral standards which he had learned from his uncle Abraham, and he didn't personally approve of the wicked things he saw and heard around him. However, as an official at the city gate, he apparently had little impact on the wicked society of which he was a part.

Peaceful co-existence is what the farmer said to the hog until hog killing day came! There can be no compromise with the flesh and the devil. What does it mean to compromise? Consider the following definitions:

1. A way of reaching agreement in which each person or group gives up something that was wanted in order to end an argument or dispute

2. Something that combines the qualities of two different things

3. A change that makes something worse and that is not done for a good reason

By these definitions we can see that compromise is not always bad. Our standard needs to be, "What does the Bible say?" Any compromise with the world, whether in doctrine, morals, or relationships, has disastrous consequences.

Compromise always will bring disastrous results for God's people. Now, before you attempt to convince me that as a mature believer you can handle anything, allow me to briefly remind you of Jehoshaphat.

In 2 Chronicles 17:3-6, we read:

"And the LORD was with Jehoshaphat, because he walked in the first ways of his father David, and sought not unto Baalim;

But sought to the LORD God of his father, and walked in his commandments, and not after the doings of Israel. Therefore the LORD stablished the kingdom in his hand; and all Judah brought to Jehoshaphat presents; and he had riches and honour in abundance. And his heart was lifted up in the ways of the LORD: moreover he took away the high places and groves out of Judah."

Jehoshaphat was a good man. He was a man of strong faith and open godliness who courageously brought reform to the nation. We would say he was an example of a mature believer. And yet, *he* suffered from the danger of compromising with the world. None of us is exempt. No one. Why did Jehoshaphat fall into the problem of compromise with the world? (Why do we compromise?)

Compromise is successful because of its subtlety. It seldom confronts us face to face. It does not reveal its real agenda, and it is quite patient.

2 Chronicles 17:1-2 tells us how Jehoshaphat strengthened his position over Israel (Ahab's northern kingdom). Later we read of his valiant army and fortified cities (17:12-19). He was ready for any attack. If Ahab had declared war, Jehoshaphat would have soundly defeated him! Instead, Ahab found a way to get his daughter married to Jehoshaphat's son. The next thing we hear is Jehoshaphat promising the godless Ahab, *"And Ahab king of Israel said unto Jehoshaphat king of Judah, Wilt thou go with me to Ramothgilead? And he answered him, I am as thou art, and my people as thy people; and we will be with thee in the war,"* (18:3)! Incredible! That's how Satan works. His attack is not usually frontal. He's tricky. He fools you with presumably good causes and lures you into his den of sin!

Wrong relationships, whether marital, social, political, business, or spiritual will destroy any believer. I imagine that when Jehoshaphat gave his son in marriage to Ahab's daughter, he thought it was for a good cause! Maybe the boy would have a positive influence on Athaliah and her mother, Jezebel! Oh, many of us fall prey to such unbiblical logic. Satan convinces us that we are strong and that *we* will be the exception to Biblical truth.

It may take time, but sin always has its consequences. Sometimes the consequences affect future generations more than our own, but if you sow compromise with the world, you will not reap God's blessings.

I know! It took twenty-seven years, but God revealed my sin. Like Lot, I too lost my position, influence, and family in order to run to the world of sexual pleasure. Why? Because at that time, that was what I wanted.

Lot surrendered his position, his influence, and his family, in order that he might live in Sodom. Why? Because that is what Lot desired.

Lot's double-mindedness brought him much inner torment and rendered him spiritually powerless. He couldn't even convince his sons-in-law (and their wives) to leave Sodom before God's judgment fell. Only he, his wife, and the two daughters still living at home escaped. His wife died instantly when she looked back, disobeying God's command. In the end, Lot lost the very things he wanted - possessions and position. This is always the case. By compromising, you will lose what you love!

2 Peter 2:7 states, "And delivered just Lot, vexed with the filthy conversation of the wicked:" The word *vexed* means to be worn down. That is what sin does. You too will be beaten down. You will not have peace. I was in such despair that I became angry following each binge of sin. Convicted by the Holy Spirit, a storm of guilt and shame raged within my soul. This is the plight of a double-souled man. It is not worth it.

As Christians, we must remember that we are engaged in spiritual warfare. To live according to God's Word requires a constant militant attitude. We need to prepare ourselves for battle. Christ has called us to be soldiers of the cross. Like Lot, we are surrounded by a corrupt, sinful society. Lot could have left Sodom and made a place for himself, his wife, and daughters where they could serve God. Instead, he accepted the status quo and stayed where he was. Consider the affect Lot's decision had on his family. When it came time to stand up for God and do right, they failed. Lot was unable to discern the danger that surrounded him. He had become spiritually impaired.

Like Lot, I chose to live in Sodom. I chose the sexual favors that were offered to me and those I sought, with no recognition of the price that would be extracted from me through suffering. In so doing, I gave Satan a foothold in my life and an opportunity for him to attack my family in a way that was possible only because of my sexual sin.

Solomon Apostas and Death
1 Kings 11:5, 33

"For Solomon went after Ashtoreth the goddess of the Zidonians, and after Milcom the abomination of the Ammonites … Because that they have forsaken me, and have worshipped Ashtoreth the goddess of the Zidonians, Chemosh the god of the Moabites, and Milcom the god of the children of Ammon, and have not walked in my ways, to do that which is right in mine eyes, and to keep my statutes and my judgments, as did David his father."

King Solomon, who followed his father King David on the throne, is known in Bible history as one of the wisest men who ever lived. Ironically, he is also known as one of history's greatest fools! Although Solomon directly knew God, actually heard God speak to him, and was greatly blessed by God, yet in his later years, he compromised the Truth with pagan trash. The trash of which I speak is humanism.

In Ecclesiastes 4:13, He may well have been talking about himself, *"Better is a poor and a wise child than an old and foolish king, who will no more be admonished."* Compromising with *what God says is right and acceptable* can require a very high price. Learn your lesson from Solomon's example. I wish that I had. I would have avoided tremendous heartbreak.

Solomon experienced blessing and success, such as the world has never seen. His downfall began with carelessness about keeping God's commands regarding idolatry. Carelessness is the first stage of lawlessness. The more careless he became, the more double-minded he became. A double-minded person loses his grip. He has difficulty choosing what he really wants. What is most important to him is not clear.

I was double-minded, (double-souled) when I walked the streets of Budapest, when I entered the massage parlor, and when I sought only the self-gratification of my flesh. Like Solomon, I tried to hold two objects, and when one began to slip, I released the one which was least important to me. The remaining object *gained control* of his mind and heart. This is a mental and spiritual battle. Therefore, take heed of Proverbs 4:23–27,

"Keep thy heart with all diligence; for out of it are the issues of life. Put away from thee a forward mouth, and perverse lips put far from thee. Let thine eyes look right on, and let thine eyelids look straight before thee. Ponder the path of thy feet, and let all thy ways be established. Turn not to the right hand nor to the left: remove thy foot from evil."

Believers must depend upon the Lord as they travel down life's road. Christ alone is able to guide us through the ditches and mine fields that Satan has prepared for us. We must crucify our flesh, for it too easily leads us to destruction. Only an intimate, personal daily walk with Christ can repel our enemy.

Solomon lost his perspective. He forgot the God *who gave him blessing and wealth,* and this led to his failure. It was actually more of a *slide* than a fall; he began to trust in his wealth and political power more than in God.

I never imagined that I would be sharing with the world the sins in which I have engaged. I suppose that Solomon thought the same thing. My slide began at the age of eleven when I was introduced to pornography by a classmate. It was new, exciting, and no one knew (or so I thought)! I was not a Christian, though I did attend church. Horrified, I watched as my father attempted to sexually abuse my mother. Many times, I tried to pull him away from my mother. I witnessed multiple illicit relationships that my father had (in my presence) before and after he divorced my mother. During my teenage years it was easy to go to the drive-in theater to seek X-rated movies. Self-gratification became sport. Even after my salvation, it seemed that I was trapped. I was faithful to church, reading the Word, and soul winning, but everything was compartmentalized. When I tried studying information about my sin, I discovered that nobody preaches about self-gratification. I found that even the church could not agree as to whether or not it was sin or an acceptable practice. Satan planted many, many seeds during my teen years.

Solomon stopped relying upon God who made all his blessing and wealth possible. With complete disregard he used his great wealth and diplomatic influence to collect a harem of 1,000 women. He disobeyed the Lord, who had told the Israelites in I Kings 11:2, *"Of the nations concerning which the LORD said unto the children of Israel, Ye shall not go in to them, neither shall they come in unto you: for surely they will turn away your heart after their gods: Solomon clave unto these in love."*

It occurred precisely according to God's Word. Solomon's many *"wives"* led him into worshipping their idols. Do we have idols in our society? Be careful how you answer this question. If I were to walk into your home, I would not necessarily see a literal altar of idols. In the Old Testament idols were made of materials such as wood, silver, gold or jewels. It was something you could see, you could handle. It was a physical expression of new devotion and commitment. Ezekiel 14:3 says, *"Son of man, **these men have set up their idols in their heart,** and put the stumbling block of their iniquity before their face: should I be inquired of at all by them?"* Idolatry then is a sin of the heart.

If idolatry were only an Old Testament sin, why then would John write, *"Little children, keep yourselves from idols. Amen"* I John 5:21.

First, we must truly understand what the word "idol" means. By definition,

1. A representation or symbol of an object of worship; *broadly:* a false god
2. A likeness of something
3. A form or appearance visible but without substance

4. An object of extreme devotion (a movie *idol*)
5. A false conception

If you try applying definition number four to your life, *"an object of extreme devotion,"* I believe that you may find many idols that lurk about, stealing away your devotion, loyalty, and faithfulness to Jesus Christ. What am I saying? Anything that comes between you and God is an idol.

Idolatry includes anything that we worship. We do not want to be controlled by sex, drugs, alcohol, food, gambling, or anything. We want to be served by our idols. However, we end up being slaves to our idols. How? Because behind every idol hiding patiently is Satan himself. God's Word reminds us, *"For we wrestle not against flesh and blood, but against principalities, against powers, against the rulers of the darkness of this world, against spiritual wickedness in high places,"* Ephesians 6:12. We are at war! To be victorious, we must rely upon the Word of God.

Solomon may have stopped short of completely rejecting the God of Israel, but he certainly compromised the truth by tolerating all sorts of paganism. He continued to offer sacrifices in the Temple, but his heart was far from God. Solomon first tolerated, then imitated. He was weak and made foolish decisions which resulted in disastrous consequences for Israel.

Is not that what we do today? This is what I did! Like Ananias and Sapphira, we mimic a commitment to God that is only for the benefit of appearance. Like Solomon, our worship becomes a mere formality, leaving our hearts lukewarm and empty. We may seek to excite ourselves through religious activity, but the true ardor of our love has been diminished by the idols that we have allowed to capture our hearts.

Samson
Judges 16
"Then went Samson to Gaza, and saw there an harlot, and went in unto her. And it was told the Gazites, saying, Samson is

come hither. And they compassed him in, and laid wait for him all
night in the gate of the city, and were quiet all the night, saying, In
the morning, when it is day, we shall kill him. And Samson lay till
midnight, and arose at midnight, and took the doors of the gate of
the city, and the two posts, and went away with them, bar and all,
and put them upon his shoulders, and carried them up to the top
of an hill that is before Hebron. And it came to pass afterward, that
he loved a woman in the valley of Sorek, whose name was Delilah.
And the lords of the Philistines came up unto her, and said unto her,
Entice him, and see wherein his great strength lieth, and by what
means we may prevail against him, that we may bind him to afflict
him: and we will give thee every one of us eleven hundred pieces
of silver. And Delilah said to Samson, Tell me, I pray thee, wherein
thy great strength lieth, and wherewith thou mightest be bound to
afflict thee. And Samson said unto her, If they bind me with seven
green withs that were never dried, then shall I be weak, and be as
another man. Then the lords of the Philistines brought up to her
seven green withs which had not been dried, and she bound him
with them. Now there were men lying in wait, abiding with her in
the chamber. And she said unto him, The Philistines be upon thee,
Samson. And he brake the withs, as a thread of tow is broken when
it toucheth the fire. So his strength was not known. And Delilah
said unto Samson, Behold, thou hast mocked me, and told me lies:
now tell me, I pray thee, wherewith thou mightest be bound. And
he said unto her, If they bind me fast with new ropes that never
were occupied, then shall I be weak, and be as another man. Delilah
therefore took new ropes, and bound him therewith, and said unto
him, The Philistines be upon thee, Samson. And there were liers in
wait abiding in the chamber. And he brake them from off his arms
like a thread. And Delilah said unto Samson, Hitherto thou hast
mocked me, and told me lies: tell me wherewith thou mightest be
bound. And he said unto her, If thou weavest the seven locks of my
head with the web. And she fastened it with the pin, and said unto
him, The Philistines be upon thee, Samson. And he awaked out of
his sleep, and went away with the pin of the beam, and with the web.

And she said unto him, How canst thou say, I love thee, when thine heart is not with me? thou hast mocked me these three times, and hast not told me wherein thy great strength lieth. And it came to pass, when she pressed him daily with her words, and urged him, so that his soul was vexed unto death; That he told her all his heart, and said unto her, There hath not come a razor upon mine head; for I have been a Nazarite unto God from my mother's womb: if I be shaven, then my strength will go from me, and I shall become weak, and be like any other man. And when Delilah saw that he had told her all his heart, she sent and called for the lords of the Philistines, saying, Come up this once, for he hath showed me all his heart. Then the lords of the Philistines came up unto her, and brought money in their hand."

A Tale of Two Minds

Samson was a Nazarite – *one set aside for God by a vow to abstain from strong drink, from shaving or cutting the hair, and from contact with a dead body.* What a study in contrasts!

Samson possessed extraordinary physical strength and is credited with remarkable exploits - the slaying of a lion and moving the gates of Gaza - before he first broke his Nazarite vow by feasting with a woman from the neighboring town of Timnah, a Philistine, one of Israel's mortal enemies.

Samson would perform other remarkable deeds. He decimated the Philistines in a private war. On another occasion, he repulsed their assault on him at Gaza, where he had gone to visit a harlot. He finally fell victim to his foes through love of Delilah, a woman of the valley of Sorek, who beguiled him into revealing the secret of his strength: *his long Nazarite hair.* As he slept, Delilah had his hair cut and betrayed him.

The Philistines put out Samson's eyes and led him, bound (with bronze chains, a type of judgment,) to Gaza. He was made to grind grain in the prison. In the East, this was usually done by women. It is obvious that such an assignment given to Samson was intended to reduce him to the lowest state of degradation and shame. (That is

Satan's way. He will take all of your strength, intellect, and ability for his own ends. When he is finished, he throws you away).

Beware, *"Be not deceived; God is not mocked: for whatsoever a man soweth, that shall he also reap. For he that soweth to his flesh shall of the flesh reap corruption; but he that soweth to the Spirit shall of the Spirit reap life everlasting,"* Galatians 6:7, 8.

During this period of imprisonment, Samson's hair began to grow, and for some reason the Philistines seemed inattentive to it. With the growing hair came a profound repentance. As he considered his sin, Samson's heart was broken, and God reinvested him with the character and powers he had lost. This is what God wants: brokenness by His children over their sin. This is a true turning to Him alone, realizing that you have no rights. This is the experiential application of Galatians 2:20, rather than superficial sentimentality in merely reciting of the verse:

"I am crucified with Christ: nevertheless I live; yet not I, but Christ liveth in me: and the life which I now live in the flesh I live by the faith of the Son of God, who loved me, and gave himself for me."

What Satan fears the most is a man (or woman), broken by the Spirit of God, who, in repentance, will throw himself upon the undeserving mercy of God.

Without a contrite heart, you will never see yourself as God sees you.

Following his denial of Christ Peter heard the cock crow, and he wept bitterly! His own heart had betrayed the One whom he loved. There must be an agreement between your spirit and God's Spirit that He is right and that you are wrong. You must also realize that your sin is first against God, and then realize how your sin has affected so many others. Do you know the extent of your influence? I suggest to you that it is greater than you know.

Satan wishes to throw you down and keep you down. He will use all that is necessary to accomplish this. Your family, your co-workers, and your church may be used to keep you in the pit of uselessness.

Praise God, we have a God of innumerable chances! When His

children come to Him in repentance, He is faithful to forgive and restore.

During a sacrificial festival to the Philistine god Dagon, Samson was brought out for entertainment. Following prayer, Samson placed his hands on pillars and brought down the building. Samson is an example to us of a man who was endowed with supernatural strength, had his faith securely placed in God, and lived in total dependence upon God.

Nevertheless, we also see a man who also acted foolishly, chronically giving in to his passions and often exercising his own will to the dishonor of God. This is what I did. I convinced myself that, because I 'only' binged every three years, I merely had a besetting sin. Do not deceive yourself as I did. Binge sinning is more than a besetting sin. It is idolatry!

Make no mistake, Samson's strength was not to be found in the length of his hair, but rather in his personal relationship with his God. It was not outward, through preaching, giving, or even soul winning, but *inward* relationship. When God looked upon his heart, he saw that his heart was one with His. This is true fellowship and worship. His uncut hair was only a mark or a sign which he wore in honor of the Lord.

One of the saddest verses in Scripture is Judges 16:20, *"And she said, The Philistines be upon thee, Samson. And he awoke out of his sleep, and said, I will go out as at other times before, and shake myself. And he wist not that the LORD was departed from him."* "He did not even realize it!

As Samson placed his hands upon the pillars of the Temple Dagon, how alone he must have felt. There was not a friendly face in the crowd, only mocking scorn. No one was there to reach out to him. No one was there with a kind word. He who was accustomed to seeing and having what he desired, now reaps what he had sown. Knowing that he was about to die, he offers a brief prayer and gives himself one last time in the service of his Master. Finally, he is singled minded. In death, he is no longer a sufferer of double-soulness.

Like Samson, your abilities to properly discern spiritual matters, to have a righteous influence upon those around you, and to stand strong, will be diminished because of your sin. It will not matter if you are a pastor, a missionary, a Christian educator, a deacon, a Sunday school teacher, or a Christian with a desire to serve the Lord. Sin is no respecter of persons! Yes, I found this out the hard way, and you will see this truth in the next chapter.

There is neither immunity nor a waiver to the sowing and reaping principle of sin. Just doing good deeds or working in a vocational ministry does not balance the ledger. James 3:1, *"My brethren, be not many masters, knowing that we shall receive the greater condemnation."*

Conversations with Brother Gabe

Dr. Brad Weniger: It's so true. We can find examples in the Bible which resemble us or our loved ones so closely that it's scary! I have to ask you, did these Bible examples convict you when you were deep in sin?

Brother Gabriel Rivera: Yes! These truths caused me great pain. There was a failure to apply these truths to my life. I battled, so I thought, but never gained victory. I sought to bring others to repentance. As a pastor, I dealt with sexual sins such as, adultery, incest, molestation, and child abuse. I knew the teaching of the Scripture. You cannot imagine the darkness and the loneliness that I felt. Driving home from a preaching engagement, I was screaming, "Lord, help me!" Someone may say, "All you had to do is apply what you knew." That is true. Then, why don't all of us do just that in every situation of life? Like the prodigal, I had to come to myself before I would seek true repentance.

Dr. Brad Weniger: How would you counsel someone like yourself in order to help them acknowledge their idolatry?

Brother Gabriel Rivera: I hope that I would counsel someone else the same way that my counselor, Pastor Mike McGee, counseled me. Brother McGee listened to me. He listened to me for hours, days, and weeks. He knew that I was in pain, but he also knew that I was not telling him the whole truth. He waited for the Holy Spirit to do His work in my heart. That day finally arrived after six weeks of counseling. It brought greater pain, but it also brought *freedom*. Any addict must first come to himself. Then he can begin to see the idols that he has built in his life.

Dr. Brad Weniger: The figures you quote for porn in the church are very disturbing. Have you found anecdotal evidence for these high numbers in your own counseling of others who have come to you seeking help?

Brother Gabriel Rivera: Unfortunately, yes, I have. Jude 22 International Ministries is a new ministry. However, every pastor that has contacted me has spoken of the needs of at least one man or more in his local church. While pastors have been hesitant to embrace this subject, they readily acknowledge the need for a ministry like Jude 22 International Ministries.

Dr. Brad Weniger: Like Samson, otherwise gifted servants of God, "strong" men and women, have fallen. What is your counsel to gifted leaders today?

Brother Gabriel Rivera: That is a difficult question. I think the best answer I can give is: "Do not mistake your giftedness or successful results in ministry as being intimate with Christ. The successes you experience may have more to do with the love of God for His people than your abilities. You must seek Christ daily for yourself, before you endeavor to use your *gifts*."

Dr. Brad Weniger: Jude 22 International Ministries is stepping up to help leaders who may have fallen. What can churches and Christians do on their own level to help the fallen whom they encounter?

Brother Gabriel Rivera: Compassion, compassion, compassion! The first thing a church or Christian can do is act with compassion. Be willing to live out Jude 22, *"And of some have compassion, making a difference."* Jude 23 describes what must be done, *"And others save with fear, pulling them out of the fire; hating even the garment spotted by the flesh."* Hate the sin, but save the sinner! Pull them out of the fire! This means *action* on our part. Passivity is not acceptable. We must take action. The recovering of men and women from sin is our responsibility. Galatians 6:1, is a clear command, *"Brethren, if a man be overtaken in a fault, ye which are spiritual, restore such an one in the spirit of meekness; considering thyself, lest thou also be tempted."* This is the work of *every church and every Christian!*

Dr. Brad Weniger: "Samson's heart was broken" and, because of his "profound repentance," "God reinvested him with the character and powers he had lost." Those are great points. They represent our sincere prayer for the fallen.

CHAPTER 5

Wither Shall I Go from Thy Spirit?

O LORD, thou hast searched me, and known me. Thou knowest my downsitting and mine uprising, thou understandest my thought afar off. Thou compassest my path and my lying down, and art acquainted with all my ways. For there is not a word in my tongue, but, lo, O LORD, thou knowest it altogether. Thou hast beset me behind and before, and laid thine hand upon me. Such knowledge is too wonderful for me; it is high, I cannot attain unto it. Whither shall I go from thy spirit? Or whither shall I flee from thy presence?
Psalm 139:1-7

All I wanted to do was park my car. My family and I were going shopping, planning to have lunch, and looking forward to a relaxing time together. It was very crowded, and I had already spent more time than I wanted to spend looking for a place to park. Then I spotted the rear lights on a car two rows over. I quickly sped around, very safely, of course, and maneuvered into position to take the parking space. From around the corner, darted a vehicle which cut me off and sped into *MY PARKING PLACE*. I was outraged. I said things that I will not repeat here. My wife and children sat in stunned silence. I wanted revenge, and I wanted it now. My family tried to calm me down, but I turned my rage toward them. "Be quiet", "I will do what I want", and on and on. By the time I was finished, or, I should say, by the time that I came to myself, no one was speaking to me. Our relaxing time had been torpedoed and sunk.

What happened? Why did I act that way? Why did I say the things that I said? I wish that I could tell you that this was just one isolated incident, but I cannot. The truth is that sin will take you farther that you ever want to go, keep you longer than you want to stay, and will cost you more than you ever want to pay. Sin will corrupt your thinking. Sin, not dealt with according to the Scripture, will become your master, even if you are saved.

Romans 6:16 says, *"Know ye not, that to whom ye yield yourselves servants to obey, his servants ye are to whom ye obey; whether of sin unto death, or of obedience unto righteousness?"*

I knew that I was saved the Bible-way, by grace through faith, from the time that I was thirteen years of age. I never doubted my salvation. I also knew that I had the best ministerial training in the world, and that my experience as an Assistant Pastor, Pastor and Missionary was second to none. God was very gracious to me and had given me great opportunity to serve Him.

I was always able to draw upon these resources in ministry, even while my personal walk with God was gravely hindered due to my periodic sexual sin, binging, pornography, and misconduct. I need to mention here, that because of both natural abilities and spiritual gifts, I did not realize my lack of intimacy with Christ. I was doing the ministry while walking in the flesh.

Galatians 5:16 – 19, is clear, *"This I say then, Walk in the Spirit, and ye shall not fulfil the lust of the flesh. For the flesh lusteth against the Spirit, and the Spirit against the flesh: and these are contrary the one to the other: so that ye cannot do the things that ye would. But if ye be led of the Spirit, ye are not under the law. Now the works of the flesh are manifest, which are these; Adultery, fornication, uncleanness, lasciviousness."*

I yielded myself to fulfill the lust of my flesh. For twenty-seven years, I led a double-life. I was miserable. I sincerely wanted God to bless me and to use me for His glory. Too often, I would stand amazed at what God was doing, not through me, but in spite of me. Because I was a binger, and not involved 24/7, I thought it would change one day, but it did not. Regardless of my war with my sexual sin, I attempted to move forward in ministry. Souls were being saved, lives changed, and Christians motivated and called to serve. I justified my personal moral lapses by focusing on outward ministry successes. I could "make it happen!"

I struggled with this for twenty-seven years. I thought that I merely had a besetting sin. I was wrong. As a sexual addict, who did not realize all the mechanics of addictions, I could not change myself. I could reach others in ministry, and yet was myself in deep spiritual distress with my own addiction. I could not minister to myself.

As for "my" successes in ministry, those were all God's successes! He honors His Word in spite of us. Isaiah 55:10, 11, *"For as the rain cometh down, and the snow from heaven, and returneth not thither, but watereth the earth, and maketh it bring forth and bud, that it may give seed to the sower, and bread to the eater: So shall my word be that goeth forth out of my mouth: it shall not return unto me void, but it shall accomplish that which I please, and it shall prosper in the thing whereto I sent it."*

So after years of a double-life, I had been "push button" programmed to just go and to press on, no matter what. That was about to all come crashing down around me. I was going to come face to face with my sin.

A Meeting is Scheduled

I was sitting in my office one day, just like any other day, (or so I thought,) when I received a visit from one of my deacons. The sign on my door read "Pastor." We were close, and he would often stop by to see how I was doing. I had been his pastor for less than one year, but we enjoyed one another's fellowship. As he sat across from me, I could tell that there was something that weighed heavily on his mind.

Finally, he asked me, "Would it be possible to meet with you on Saturday morning? There are some things that Cindy and I have been discussing, and I would like to talk them over with you."

He was quite vague about the purpose of the meeting, and so I tried to ask a few questions. "Is there anything that I can do today? Are you and Cindy all right?"

"No, there isn't anything really urgent. We are okay. I just thought we should see you."

I replied, "Well, my wife and I will be glad to sit down with both of you."

Confronting My Sin

When Saturday morning arrived, I anticipated that my wife and I would both go to the church office. However, she was not sure, and, just as we began discussing her participation, my phone rang. It was my deacon calling to let me know that he would be a few minutes late, and that his wife would not be joining us. That was curious! I was concerned and confused, but I said goodbye to my wife and left for my office.

The parking lot was empty except for Bob's car. He was waiting for me in the foyer. I thought it was odd, because he had just called me to say that he would be late. Anyway, we went into my office and sat down. I could tell that Bob was very uncomfortable. We prayed together, and I asked, "Bob, how can I help you? Is Cindy going to be joining us later?"

It was as if he had not heard me nor registered my concern.

He responded, "Pastor, this is very difficult for me. Your wife has been sharing with Cindy some alarming information concerning you for several weeks. Pastor, your wife is quite distraught!"

"Bob, what are you talking about? What concerns? What did she say?"

It was at that very moment someone knocked on my door. "Come in," I said. When the door opened, it was my wife, and behind her was our son. I just stared at them in bewilderment. To say that I was in shock is an understatement. My breathing became inexplicably rapid. Finally, I asked, "Why are you here?" I did not know what to ask nor to whom I should speak. The four of us just stood there in silence.

The date on my calendar read July 2, 2011. I thought that my deacon and his wife needed help. I had even commented to my wife during the week that we needed to be in prayer for Bob and Cindy. I was truly concerned. I was completely unaware of the real reason for the meeting.

I felt absolutely alone. I was experiencing Psalm 139. Indeed where could I go? How could I have been so foolish as to think God did not know of my sin? *"Yea, the darkness hideth not from thee; but the night shineth as the day: the darkness and the light are both alike to thee"* Psalm 139:12.

The secret haunts of sin are as open before God as the most brash and loudmouthed bully. My mind was replaying where I had been and what I had done.   As I returned to my chair behind my desk, I thought, "Lord, I want to die." I was the Preacher, the Pastor. How could I have sinned against my Lord, my wife, and my church this way? My son brought in two more chairs from the foyer. We all sat.

Bob broke the stony silence, "Pastor, this is about you." Bob continued, "Pastor, your wife has shared with Cindy that she has found pornography on your home computer, and that this is not the first time."

I was crushed, speechless, and ashamed. I was afraid. I felt empty and very alone. I could not find my voice. I tried to process what had just been said, and I knew that it was true. I *had* been viewing pornography, and I had visited chat rooms. I was being publically exposed.

I did what most do when they are "busted," I attempted to blame shift, to deflect the severity of my sin. I exclaimed, "I have a besetting sin. I am trying to have victory."

Every word that came out of my mouth was hollow and defensive. I was caught! I was broken, but not by the Lord. I was experiencing a worldly sorrow. I was thinking of myself. If I had to leave the ministry how would I survive? Where would we live? How much do I confess to at this time? I am an independent Baptist. Who in the world will even want to help me?

I was acutely aware of the prevailing sentiment among *Fundamentalists* concerning a sinning brother or sister. Specifically, *we frequently shoot our own wounded.* Oh, it was always mentioned with a smile or shared as a feeble attempt at humor, but I knew that

I had become a spiritual leper. I knew the truth. I was now a statistic to be quoted.

The longer we sat there the more I knew that I needed help. However, what I did not realize was how much help, and what type of help, I would truly need.

Bob interrupted my thoughts, "Pastor, I need to hear from you that what your wife is saying *is* true."

There was it seemed an eternity of silence. Finally I answered, "Yes, it is true."

I had just confessed to my wife, to my son, and to my deacon and friend that I was guilty of participating in internet pornography. I had no idea what the future looked like or if I even had a future. "What do I do? Where do I go? Who can help me? Will anyone want to help me?"

Then the discussion turned to my ability to preach the next day. I assured everyone that I would be fine. It was getting late, and I thought it would be too great of an imposition to call someone for pulpit supply.

I thought to myself, "I want to preach. It may be the last time I am allowed to preach." It was also the Fourth of July weekend. There would be guests present. I wanted to be in the pulpit.

As I pleaded my case, I mentioned that my wife and I would get through this. I will submit to counseling. It was at that point that my wife let me know that she was *leaving*.

"What do you mean leaving?" I asked.

She said, "I am afraid of you. I do not want to stay here because I am afraid of what you might do when we get home?"

The deacon interrupted, "Mrs. Rivera, you do not need to leave. Please, if you do not feel safe come and stay with Cindy and me."

"No, I have already made arrangements with my daughter. She is here from out of state, and I am going to go home with her."

Everything in the room began spinning as my wife's words penetrated my heart. I went out to the foyer, and there sat our daughter. I had no idea that she was present. I began to weep. Bitter tears flowed from my eyes. I was numb.

I began to beg my wife not to leave. I said that I would leave the house if she did not feel safe. "Please stay. I will go to counseling. Stay with Bob and Cindy, but do not leave." Nothing that I could say made any difference. Our daughter took her to our home to get the rest of her things. She left.

My son and my deacon agreed that I should not preach. A former pastor was called to fill the pulpit. Several names of biblical counselors were discussed. I agreed that I would contact one immediately on Monday.

A good friend for over twenty years had been called by my son to see if he would come and spend some time with me. Though my family was concerned that I should not be left alone, they did not want to be with me.

My deacon said, "Pastor, I am so sorry. We will get through this and I will do anything that I can to help you." We wept.

My son waited for my friend John to arrive. There was little conversation. When John arrived, he hugged me, and we sat down to talk. My son said goodbye.

I am blessed to have had a number of close friends. Later, I will introduce another one of my friends, but now I want you to meet John. A friend is one who is faithful, loyal, kind, unselfish, steadfast, and one who strengthens you spiritually. These are precious, priceless and, rare. John is such a friend.

An Arab Proverb identifies the type of man who is your friend.

"Ah, the beauty of being at peace with another, neither having to weigh thoughts or measure words, but spilling them out just as they are, chaff and grain together, certain that a faithful hand will keep what is worth keeping, and with a breath of kindness blow the rest away."

We had been friends through both joys and trials. He had always been there for me, and I would like to believe that I have been there for him as well. Contrary to what my family believes about John, he always told me precisely what I needed to hear, not merely what I wanted to hear. That is a mark of friendship.

As I began to recount what was going, on he stopped me.

He said, "I already know what is happening here. Your son called me earlier and told me that there was going to be a meeting. They (your family) are afraid that you might try to hurt yourself, and they knew that you would talk to me."

The fact that he was informed earlier that day about the meeting pushed me further into despair. Everything seemed so hopeless. I began to view suicide as a plausible solution to my situation. "No one would miss me. No one would care. The pain, and disappointments would come to an end!"

It seemed that everyone knew about today – everyone except me! I had been living in my own little world, wrapped up in my sin, *which I thought was secret.* Slowly, I had lost my discernment and sensitivity to everything and to everyone around me.

I want to be clear about my confession. It did not come quickly nor easily. It did not come without first pointing out the sins of my wife. It did not come without my trying to explain and to minimize my sin. That is what Satan can do to anyone who does not have an intimate relationship with Jesus Christ. That's what Satan did *to me.*

Selfishness, deception, and blaming others for "not understanding you" become your defense, but there is no true defense. Over the next two years, I would discover that nothing can save a man or woman from sexual addiction if they are not willing to REPENT!

You must be willing to forsake everything and everyone in order to follow only Christ! Unfortunately, as you will see in the succeeding chapters, I was not yet finished with my lies! I was sorry, but it was only a worldly sorrow. Oh, how the Lord was going to deal with my heart! I was filled with despair. I needed Biblical hope.

Conversations with Brother Gabe

Dr. Brad Weniger: Let's talk about your anger problem while you were living a double-life. That was a symptom wasn't it?

Brother Gabriel Rivera: Yes, it was. We all know that fear is a powerful emotion. Whether consciously or unconsciously, I needed to hide my fear, of being caught. I needed to be right all the time. I needed to be in control all the time. I was afraid of being less than what people believed I was. I see now that I used anger to control and to manipulate people. If you ask me about my past, I would tell you that my world glorified anger as a tool. However, if I would have grown in Christ, He would have taken away my anger. The fruit that God has given me since my repentance is, I am no longer a slave to anger. YOU cannot make me angry. I was such a fool trying to live my way rather than giving all of myself to Christ.

Dr. Brad Weniger: Your anger was a symptom of what?

Brother Gabriel Rivera: A much, much worse problem. My hair trigger anger should have sent a signal that there was deeper trouble. It is sad, but Christians more often than not are satisfied to say, "Hi, how are you today?" as they pass you in the hallway. I am not blaming anyone. I am stating the facts. We really do not want to get involved with one another. However, the Scriptures clearly teach that we have a responsibility to one another. We are to comfort, admonish, edify, exhort, love, be kind to, forgive, forbear, and teach one another!

Dr. Brad Weniger: Are sexual addicts (and other addicts) often in denial?

Brother Gabriel Rivera: Absolutely! I lived with seventy men for seven months in a program for sexual addiction. I never had one tell me that they knew they had a problem. They believed that they could control their sexual desires, just as I believed that I could control my desires. We were all wrong!

Dr. Brad Weniger: This anger problem, which was symptomatic, later proved to be a hindrance to reconciliation, didn't it?

Brother Gabriel Rivera: True. My wife was afraid of me. I wanted to have our marriage restored, and she was certain that I was out to kill her.

Dr. Brad Weniger: How ironic! That's what Satan does when we lay ourselves open to him by our sin. Of course, professionals cleared you of any wrong doing.

Brother Gabriel Rivera: Absolutely. She must have been terrified, but there was never any effort nor any threat to harm her, and there was no evidence whatsoever. Just the opposite.

Dr. Brad Weniger: What a shock to your system when your sin was exposed! You *were* busted," weren't you?

Brother Gabriel Rivera: Although I had a loving God and a dear friend, I felt abandoned. Of course, I did that to myself. Now I regret that the church and the Christian community didn't know how to deal with me and with my poor family. How they have suffered!

Dr. Brad Weniger: Just about everyone scattered, didn't they? And that's really why Jude 22 International Ministries was born. Fallen folks need someone to come near and to really care.

CHAPTER 6

Long Road to Repentance

"For godly sorrow worketh repentance to salvation not to be repented of: but the sorrow of the world worketh death." 2 Corinthians 7:10

Sunday, July 3, 2011, was a continuation of despair, grief, hopelessness, and despondency. Emotionally, I was a train wreck. Physically, I was vomiting. Spiritually, I was deaf and dumb. I was alone with my thoughts. My flesh cried out as replay after replay of my sin overloaded my memory.

Psalm 38:2-14 is the appropriate description of that day.

"For thine arrows stick fast in me, and thy hand presseth me sore.

There is no soundness in my flesh because of thine anger; neither is there any rest in my bones because of my sin. For mine iniquities are gone over mine head: as an heavy burden they are too heavy for me.

My wounds stink and are corrupt because of my foolishness. I am troubled; I am bowed down greatly; I go mourning all the day long. For my loins are filled with a loathsome disease: and there is no soundness in my flesh. I am feeble and sore broken: I have roared by reason of the disquietness of my heart.

Lord, all my desire is before thee; and my groaning is not hid from thee. My heart panteth, my strength faileth me: as for the light of mine eyes, it also is gone from me. My lovers and my friends stand aloof from my sore; and my kinsmen stand afar off. They also that seek after my life lay snares for me: and they that seek my hurt speak mischievous things, and imagine deceits all the day long.

But I, as a deaf man, heard not; and I was as a dumb man that openeth not his mouth. Thus I was as a man that heareth not, and in whose mouth are no reproofs."

Even while the Spirit of God was attempting to draw me back to Himself, I found myself scheming. Yes, the pain I was experiencing was real. However, there is a difference between shame and brokenness. You can experience shame for various and sundry reasons. Examples include shame for simply being "busted," or shame because you lost something or someone. Being disgraced, humiliated, or embarrassed does not automatically bring brokenness. It brings, as Paul said, *"the sorrow of the world."*

Shame will make you sorry, but only brokenness will bring you to God. To be broken is to relinquish all of your rights to God, and to stop trying to do everything your own way. Cry out to God for mercy, and acknowledge your need for renewal and cleansing. Plead for forgiveness. This is what David was doing in Psalm 51:17: *"The sacrifices of God are a broken spirit: a broken and a contrite heart, O God, thou wilt not despise."*

In the midst of pain, I was still scheming. Why? I knew that I was guilty of more than internet pornography. I was guilty of chronic adultery! I had an appointment to see a Biblical counselor. I was thinking, "What would I tell him? Is it possible to save my position? What type of job could I possibly find? How much would it pay?"

Before God can deliver us from ourselves we must undeceive ourselves. - Augustine

I really did not know if I could share my sin with anyone. So I did not. Again, the Lord showed His great love for me in sending me to a patient and discerning Biblical counselor. He spent hours listening to my pathetic attempts to hide behind (what I termed) "a besetting sin."

I am ashamed to say that it took almost six weeks before I

confessed my adultery. I really did not fully comprehend what repentance looked like. I was sad, but not repentant. I wanted the situation to change, but I thought I had only a small problem. I was still doing everything in the flesh by saying and doing the correct things, and by completing the assignments given to me by my Biblical counselor. Yet, I knew that I was lying to him.

Following one of our sessions, we prayed together, and I got up to leave.

As I walked toward the door, I felt pressure upon my shoulders. I stopped, turned around, and said, "I have been lying to you."

My counselor responded, "I know that you have been."

I walked back to his office, and I began weeping as I opened my heart. It was not my intention to confess more than I had. I was "scheming"! I was trying to admit only that which I thought was necessary. Why? I was afraid of losing my wife and family. "If I confess all of my sin," I reasoned, "they will never forgive me. I will never be able to preach again. I will become an outcast with no one to stand by me." Basically, I did not trust my Lord.

As I confessed to my acts of chronic adultery, I looked up, and I said, "I am going to have to tell my wife, right?"

My counselor replied, "What do you think?"

I knew that I had to confess it all. God was giving me the opportunity to be free. The only way to be free is to tell the truth. It is impossible to build a new relationship on a lie or half-truth. Regardless of the consequences, my wife needed to know that I loved her enough to risk everything by telling her the whole truth.

I continued in counseling on a weekly basis for almost two months. During this time, the Lord was faithful to keep me humbled. As the days passed, it became apparent that I needed more than just a new job and once a week counseling. So when my counselor suggested a live-in program for sexual addictions, I agreed to take a look at it. It would mean leaving everyone. It was a six to twelve month program. I had to be willing to "give up" one year of my life if that is what the Lord desired. I rationalized, "What is one year after twenty-seven years of bondage?" I did not like who I was. During those years, I wanted to change, but I never did. I believed that this was my last opportunity.

Several weeks after confessing my chronic adultery to my counselor, I met with my wife and her counselor. She was crushed. I broke her heart all over again. I left out no details. I wept as I begged her to forgive me. As I offered a complete confession, I was acutely aware that any attempt at future reconciliation may never be realized, but I was through scheming. Whatever happened, I needed to trust the Lord and do it His way.

That was August 16, 2011. As of this writing, I have only seen my wife three times since that day. *"You can choose your sin, but you cannot choose the consequences of your sin."* I had heard this statement many, many times during my ministry. Now I knew its truth and pain experientially. Sin offends our holy God and separates us from Him. Sin is disobeying God, including unintended wrongdoing. Sin is in our nature and must be faced by every individual.

I listened to my counselor and made application to a live-in program for my sexual addiction. Between July 2, 2011, and September 1, 2011, I had lost everything, including my wife, my family, my position, my influence, and my hope. Sin is not to be taken lightly. Especially beware of so-called hidden sins. They will slowly, but surely destroy you, as illustrated by this story:

When Leonardo da Vinci was painting his masterpiece, The Last Supper, he selected as the person to sit for the character of the Christ a young man, Pietri Bandinelli by name, connected with the Milan Cathedral as chorister. Years passed before the great picture was completed, and when one character only - that of Judas Iscariot—was wanting, the great painter noticed a man in the streets of Rome whom he selected as his model. With shoulders far bent toward the ground, having an expression of cold, hardened, evil, saturnine, the man seemed to afford the opportunities of a model terribly true to the artist's conception of Judas. When in the studio, the profligate began to look around, as if recalling incidents of years gone by. Finally, he turned and with a look half-sad, yet one which told how hard it was to realize the change which had taken place, he said, "Maestro, I was in this studio twenty-five years ago. I, then, sat for Christ."

I was accepted by a live-in program and was told to arrive on September 12, 2011. My feet were attempting to walk the road of repentance. It would prove to be a very long road. Ambrose of Milan said, *"True repentance is to cease from sin."* I had not been able to cease in twenty-seven years. Why? What was wrong with me? Knowing what I knew, how could I sin this way? As much pain as I was experiencing, it was about to get much worse. God meant business. Now the question before me was, "Do I want what He is offering me?"

Conversations with Brother Gabe

Dr. Brad Weniger: It sounds like there's a huge amount of *carnal remorse* in this world with far less *true repentance*. Is that what you believe based on your own personal experience?

Brother Gabriel Rivera: *Remorse* and *regret* are often mistaken for repentance. They are not the same. Like small children with cookies crumbs around their mouths, so is the sorrow of the addict. He got "busted," but he does not change his mind about enjoying the cookies. Regret implies feeling uneasy about the past or present. The example of this is found in Matthew 27:3 *"Then Judas, which had betrayed him, when he saw that he was condemned, repented himself, and brought again the thirty pieces of silver to the chief priests and elders."* Here **repented** means remorse or regret which leads to death. Repentance is an action which leads to change. *Repentance* implies coming to a right mind. Unfortunately, I do believe that there is a huge number of people who experience remorse, but who fall short of *true repentance*. I was such a person.

Dr. Brad Weniger: You said, "Shame will make you sorry, but only brokenness will bring you to God." Do you believe that God permitted you to be *broken?*

Brother Gabriel Rivera: Yes, I believe that God was, literally turning my world inside out. This was God's mercy!

Dr. Brad Weniger: In your own words describe what it felt like to be broken.

Brother Gabriel Rivera: The word *broken* means *not functioning properly; out of working order.* That is how I felt. I could not function. Simple tasks drained my energy and became extremely time consuming. Routine decisions seemed foreign to me. This was only the beginning. During six weeks of Biblical counseling God continued chiseling away at the "straw man" that I had built. God was taking me apart and showing me the pieces. God was taking away everyone and everything that I loved. God wanted my complete attention. Two weeks after I arrived at the live-in program for sexual addiction, God gave me the gift of seeing myself as He saw me. The result of that experience was great emotional, physical, and spiritual pain. God opened my eyes. God showed me my heart. I did not like what I saw.

Dr. Brad Weniger: Are you *still* broken now, and why is that a "good thing"?

Brother Gabriel Rivera: Being broken, is indeed, a good thing. I am constantly reminded that I have no rights. I learned this through the pain of my self-inflicted wounds. David, in Psalm 51:3 says, *"For I acknowledge my transgressions: and my sin is ever before me."* David had such a deep sense of his sin, that he could not stop thinking about it, through the lens of sorrow and shame. Sorrow and shame serve to remind me how my God sees my sin and how my sin affected so many people. Brokenness and humility are twins. I am humbled that God loves me and wants to give me another chance. When the Lord revealed to me the pride that I possessed, that also brought brokenness and humility.

Dr. Brad Weniger: You say you were self-deceived. Why?

Brother Gabriel Rivera: I say I was self-deceived, because I denied the significance of my actions. I began rationalizing away the relevance of what I was doing. I convinced myself that I had only a *besetting sin,* and, as such, was not responsible.

Dr. Brad Weniger: It was not easy confessing *all* your sin. What was it like telling your wife *everything?*

Brother Gabriel Rivera: I knew that I needed to confess *everything* to my wife. I knew that there was a possibility that she would want a divorce. What I was not prepared for was the expression of pain on her face. Immediately, I was acutely aware of the depth of my sin against her. I will never forget that day. As a man, we compartmentalize things in our thinking. We can convince ourselves that what we are doing in one area of our life, really doesn't affect other areas of our life. I did that. It is a lie! Every area of our life affects everyone around us.

Dr. Brad Weniger: How true it is that "you can choose your sin, but you cannot choose the consequences of your sin." Are you *still* experiencing those consequences?

Brother Gabriel Rivera: Yes, I am, and I will for the rest of my life. Again, Psalm 51:3b says, *"...my sin is ever before me."* I experience this in practical ways. A trip to the grocery store, for example, becomes emotionally painful when I see my wife's favorite cereal. I am sitting in church on Grandparents' Day alone, knowing that I am not allowed to see my grandchildren. Former friends in ministry no longer have time for me. I could give you many examples, but I won't. I understand that each individual is responsible for how they interact with a repentant sinner. I believe that is exactly what I am: a repentant sinner. My sin was personal, intimate, and deceitful. I pray that the Lord would keep my heart soft and pliable. I want to be available so that my Lord can use me if He so desires.

Dr. Brad Weniger: May God use your solemn warning to deter others from their sin!

Brother Gabriel Rivera: Amen!

DOUBLE-SOUL

CHAPTER 7

Will the Real Pharisee Stand Up?

Sunday night September 11, 2011, was the longest night of my life. I said good-bye to my wife around 7:30 p.m., not realizing, that I would see her just one more time in the next two and a half years. I traveled by bus through the night. I felt alone and very much out of place. The bus was older, crowded, and noisy. It seemed as if we stopped every forty minutes. Finally, we arrived in Kentucky at 10:00 a.m., Monday, September 12, 2011.

Sleep was not my companion, haunted by the memories of what brought me to this moment in my life. It was storming as we drove through the mountains. I thought to myself, "How symbolic this is of my life!" The pounding thunder of Satan's laughter and the sharp lightning flashes of his demons, dancing in celebration of their victory, evoked thoughts of my death. I was sure that I was finished!

At this point, I was an emotional, spiritual, and mental invalid. Perhaps you have been there, or are there now. I was no longer in control, nor was my opinion of any value, nor did I have any real sense of purpose. As I wrestled with my thoughts, my phone rang. It was my son calling. Because of the storm, we could barely hear each other. A while later, my oldest daughter called while I was in Tennessee on a very long layover. She said, "Dad, I love you. We will get through this." She called several times during that night, assuring me of her love and forgiveness. As of this writing, I have not heard the voices of my son nor my older daughter since that night. I had never felt so totally abandoned, isolated, and utterly alone. That is what sin does to you!

Again, let me shout from the house tops Galatians 6:7, 8: *"Be not deceived; God is not mocked: for whatsoever a man soweth, that shall he also reap. For he that soweth to his flesh shall of the flesh reap corruption; but he that soweth to the Spirit shall of the Spirit reap life everlasting."*

Though I did not understand it that night, God was showing me how much He loved me. We often think of God's love in terms of sunshine and blessing, or health and prosperity. God was showing me His loving hand in discipline. Think about it! God can do anything that He wants to do. He could have taken me out of this world. In fact, I begged Him to do just that! "Take me home Lord," I had cried out during the twenty-seven years of lies, sin, and deception so many times that I cannot count them.

I awoke the next morning, exhausted. My attempt to convince God to remove me from this world had failed. Now, as I sat at the bus station waiting to be picked up, I wondered, "Where am I? How am I going to get through this?" I waited for more than an hour for someone from the rehabilitation ministry to arrive.

When the gentleman finally showed up, he explained, "You were supposed to call the ministry when you started your trip. When we did not hear from you, we were not sure that you were actually coming." He said, "We have a lot of men who pay the $2,000.00 induction fee, but then never show up."

What? I had never even entertained the thought of *not showing up*. Actually filled with fear, I wondered what I would do had I not been accepted? I knew that I could not 'fix' myself. Whatever the Lord had planned for me at this ministry, I knew that I needed it, and so I wanted to be there.

There was very little conversation on the way to the Ranch. I was tired, scared, and wondering what this next year would bring. Even though I longed for deliverance, it was still a daunting step to imagine a six to twelve month program. Leave all of your thoughts, plans, rights, and desires at the door!

I was escorted to a dormitory, appropriately called "Lazarus"! I needed to be resurrected from the death of sexual sin. Lazarus would be my home for the next six weeks. There were sixteen men sleeping in bunk beds, and all lights had to be out at 10:00 p.m. I was given the name of my counselor, and I was informed that he would meet with me at 2:00 p.m.

My counselor explained what would be expected of me while at the Ranch. On Monday and Wednesday nights there were prayer groups. Tuesday night was accountability night. On Thursdays, there were testimonies, praise, and preaching. On Friday nights, there were preaching videos, note taking required, and notes and homework were to be turned in to your counselor. Each Saturday night featured either another teaching video or an inspirational film. Church services were conducted on the grounds at 10:00 a.m. on Sundays. One Sunday a month, we visited a local church. I would be assigned a weekly chore that was to be completed each day. Once or twice a month, I would be assigned kitchen cleanup. I would be given the opportunity to work outside the Ranch for $8.50 to $9.00 per hour. As I left my counselor, I attempted to assimilate all that he had shared. I recall thinking, "This is going to be the hardest thing that I have ever faced. I don't know if I can do this Lord. Please, please help me!" I went to my bunk, buried my head, and wept!

There were many, many defining moments during my seven month stay at the Ranch. God was using everything and everyone around me to point me to an intimate relationship with Jesus Christ. I was coming face to face with that which was lacking in my life: an intimate, first love relationship with Jesus Christ! There was nothing too small nor insignificant. I want to share three of these moments with you.

On September 24, twelve days after my arrival, God and I had a personal meeting in the chapel. It was Saturday night. I was crushed by the weight of my sin. Question after question pounded inside my head. I looked around, and I saw men who were guilty of every sexual sin that one can imagine. I thought, "I do not belong here. I am not like them." I wondered about my own salvation. I cried. I screamed. I sobbed openly. I wanted - *I needed to know* - "How could I? Why did I? Who am I?" And, "What have I done to my family?" I was desperate.

I prayed, "Lord, I see that I have wasted twenty-seven years, many times walking in the flesh. I was selfish. I was proud. If I am not your child, if I am not saved, oh, please save me! I want to settle this tonight. I give myself to you. No longer do I want to walk in the flesh, but I want to walk in the Spirit. Please, Lord, help me!"

For hours I cried out, seeking the Lord. Without a specific thought or plan, I prayed, "Lord, please let me see my heart the way You see it." And the Lord answered my prayer. Immediately, I was broken. I saw the wickedness of all of my sin. I trembled and shook at what I saw. He clearly showed me that my sin was first and foremost against my Savior. God gave me a wonderful gift that night! A gift that has *kept* me broken and repentant.

A great peace filled my soul as I realized how much Christ loved me. He loved me enough to reveal my sexual sin. He put me in a place which I never would have chosen on my own. This place did not care about my ministry, but only cared about me "pressing into Jesus Christ." Christ loved me enough to allow me to experience the pain of my disobedience that, in turn, I might come to Him.

Everything that I read and every message that I heard pierced my soul. I was meeting with my counselor once a week. He assigned special books to be read and Scripture to be memorized. After we had a guest preacher come for special meetings, my counselor asked me what I thought about the messages. I explained that I thought they were excellent, inspiring, and encouraging, but I could tell that I was not giving him the answer he was seeking.

Finally, he looked at me and asked, "Is that all...? Just inspiring, encouraging...? You are a Pharisee!" He shouted at me.

I did not know how to reply. I had been honest. I had told him truthfully how I felt. I sat in stunned silence. A Pharisee? What did he mean? I was "humble." I always thought of others. I had given my life in full-time vocational ministry. How could he say this to me? I wanted to run away. I wanted to leave the program. A Pharisee! I had no money, no car, and no place to go. I left his office angry, confused, and I was determined to leave. I saw the director and tried to approach him, but he ignored me. I was alone! I had no one to talk to, no one to soothe my hurt feelings, no one ... and that was the answer. God wanted me to turn to Him alone. He had me right where He wanted me to be. ALONE! I had no lifeline nor safety net.

As I began crying out to the Lord, I turned to the passage in Luke 18:10-14:

"Two men went up into the temple to pray; the one a Pharisee, and the other a publican. The Pharisee stood and prayed thus with himself, God, I thank thee, that I am not as other men are, extortionist, unjust, adulterers, or even as this publican. I fast twice in the week, I give tithes of all that I possess. And the publican, standing afar off, would not lift up so much as his eyes unto heaven, but smote upon his breast, saying, God be merciful to me a sinner. I tell you, this man went down to his house justified rather than the other: for every one that exalteth himself shall be abased; and he that humbleth himself shall be exalted."

As I read about the Pharisee, I realized that my counselor was correct. Though I had been at the Ranch for exactly one month, I was still in a state of shock and awe. As I had listened to other men give accounts of their sexual sin and what brought them to the Ranch, what were my thoughts?

"Lord, I really do not belong here. I am thankful that I am not like these other men. They are addicts. I am a binger. I am not a 24/7 sexual addict. I have not done what these men have done. I .... ." My excuses stopped. I ceased beating my chest when I realized and admitted that I, indeed, was a PHARISEE!

I ran outside to the prayer trail. Weeping in disbelief, I found myself at the foot of the cross. I knelt and raised my sinful, disobedient, Pharisaical hands to God and begged Him to forgive me. At that moment, I knew that I was just like the men around me. I was a sex addict, and could not deliver myself.

One of the assigned books which I had read was *From Pride to Humility* by Stuart Scott. Other than the Word of God, this book did more in revealing my heart to me than anything else. During my three week study, I came to the conclusion that of the thirty manifestations of pride, I possessed at least twenty-two! I had so many areas to confront. Mine was much more than just a besetting sin. These included: complaining against God; blame-shifting (why didn't God deliver me? why didn't my wife help me? why didn't my pastor who knew about my internet pornography do something?); being sarcastic; being deceitful by covering up sins, fault, mistakes. As I addressed each manifestation, the Lord faithfully and painfully revealed who I was.

During my next counseling session, I confessed that God had revealed to me that indeed I was a *Pharisee*. This was a turning point for me.

I wonder, friend, have you found your turning point? It is not easy to come to terms with sin which you thought was hidden. I confess to you, that, had I known ahead of time the pain that would be mine when I asked the Lord to allow me to see my heart as He saw it, I would never have uttered that prayer. However, I am thankful that my God gives me exactly what I need. He knew that my habitual sin of twenty-seven years would not be relinquished easily. He knew the radical steps that I would need to take in order to break the cycle of sin that controlled me. He who knows all things gave me exactly what I needed to begin my long journey of repentance.

And He was not finished!

Conversations with Brother Gabe

Dr. Brad Weniger: Were you insulted and offended when your counselor called you a Pharisee? Do you think you were thin skinned about it?

Brother Gabriel Rivera: Let me say here, that I was very, very thankful for my counselor. He did not allow me to wallow in self-pity. He was direct with me. He pointed me to the Scriptures. He prayed for me. I know that he loved me. He loved me enough, knowing that I was a Pharisee to tell me that I was a Pharisee. Yet, I was offended. I could not believe it. I was hurt. I understand what a Pharisee is, and I was sure that I was not a Pharisee! I was *wrong*. My counselor helped me to learn to submit to authority. He helped me to see that it is not about being right, being first, or being the best. It is about being obedient and submissive to the Lord in every area of my life.

Dr. Brad Weniger: You talk about needing to be *alone* without "a lifeline or a safety net." Do you think we sometimes artificially "prop up" sinners in their sin just because we feel badly for them or their situation?

Brother Gabriel Rivera: I really do think that the church is guilty of artificially "propping up" sinners. It is easy to see a sinner's situation and to think, *"They are suffering enough. I am not going to add to their suffering by pointing out their sin."* While the suffering may be severe, there is no excuse for not following the Biblical model in dealing with sin. We do not demonstrate God's love by being disobedient to His Word. We can be loving and still hold people accountable. This is true especially when dealing with addicts. Years before, when my internet pornography was first revealed, I believe that it would have been helpful had I been asked to step out of ministry in order to deal with my sin.

Dr. Brad Weniger: You say you discovered twenty-two manifestations of pride, and, when you addressed each of these manifestations of pride, "the Lord faithfully and painfully" revealed who you were. That was *a turning point* for Gabe Rivera. Because you've shared this painful experience, what do you hope it will do for others?

Brother Gabriel Rivera: I want people to know that they are not alone. I Corinthians 10:13 is true, *"There hath no temptation taken you but such as is common to man: but God is faithful, who will not suffer you to be tempted above that ye are able; but will with the temptation also make a way to escape, that ye may be able to bear it."* It is my hope that the people who read this book will be convicted of and will turn away from their sin. I pray that they will recognize that there is hope in Jesus Christ. I pray that men and women will realize that there is an organization, Jude 22 International Ministries, which will compassionately pick them up, hold them up, and build them up. This will take time and effort. Pride is a deceitful and powerful enemy. Do you have an issue with pride? How do you know? Here are several manifestations.

1. Perfectionism – People who strive for everything to be perfect often do so for recognition.
2. A lack of admitting when you are wrong – A proud person will make many excuses.
3. Not having close relationships – Proud people often have no use for close relationships.
4. Being devastated or angered by criticism – Proud people usually struggle a great deal with criticism.

CHAPTER 8

What Does Repentance Look Like?

As fall turned to winter, my soul was learning what it means to "walk out your repentance." For so many years, I was consumed with *doing* rather than with *being*. I came to understand that we can recognize the problems that stem from our carnal nature and attack them vigorously, but we fail to realize that we are merely attacking the symptoms. We fail to recognize the root of our carnality. What is our solution? What do we do? We who are fundamentalists, run to engage in more activity. We do things! Some of the things we do are not necessarily wrong. Repenting, praying, growing, maturing, and trying to live in humility are good things to do. However, we never seem to break through into that abundant life that John 10:10 speaks about, *"The thief cometh not, but for to steal, and to kill, and to destroy: I am come that they might have life, and that they might have it more abundantly."* Something is not exactly "right." It's not the way we would like it to be. The problem is, WE STILL WANT TO BE IN CONTROL OF OUR LIFE.

Until we are willing to "be" Galatians 2:20 toward all people, *"I am crucified with Christ: nevertheless I live; yet not I, but Christ liveth in me: and the life which I now live in the flesh I live by the faith of the Son of God, who loved me, and gave himself for me,"* we will never know what it means to experience the abundant life. Paul said, I am dead. I no longer live. Listen to me, dead men and women have no rights. Dead men and women have no strength.

Dead men and women are not self-sufficient. They are *dead!*

Repentance begins with our death to our own thinking, to our own desires, and to our own plans. It seeks to minister to the needs of those around us. It seeks first the kingdom of God and His righteousness by setting our affection on things above, and by looking unto Jesus the author and finisher of our faith. Mrs. Lot, do not look back. Do *not* look back! There is *nothing* "back there" for you.

The New Unger's Bible Dictionary defines repentance as containing three essential elements. (1) A genuine sorrow toward God on account of sin; (2) an inward repugnance to sin necessarily followed by the actual forsaking of it: and (3) a humble self-surrender to the will and service of God.

Personally, I had embraced the most elementary stage of repentance, fear of the consequences of sin. Going no further, I was trapped by remorse, but not yet experiencing a godly sorrow (2 Corinthians 7:9, 10).

Friends, if you only desire freedom from your addictions or hang-ups so that you can be a better pastor, youth leader, worship leader, Sunday school teacher, husband, wife, parent, friend, whatever, then your heart is not right before God, nor are your intentions. Freedom comes only when we see ourselves in the pure light of God's holiness, and we desire nothing more or less than to be in fellowship with him.

Let me say a word here about what repentance is NOT. **Repentance is not being sorry that your life is a mess because of your mistakes.** For many years I cried out to God to help me stop doing the things I was doing, but my motives were selfish. I was fearful that I might lose my family, my job, or that someone "important" might find out. I was even sorry that my work in the ministry, in which I took great pride, might be hampered by my sinful choices made in secret.

Many Christians, particularly those in some form of ministry, want freedom from their addiction to pornography or self-gratification, because they sense that it is preventing them from being all that they could be in their vocation. **This is not repentance, but is** spiritual pride. A great example of this is found in Acts 8 in the story of Simon the Magician.

"Thy money perish with thee, because thou hast thought that the gift of God may be purchased with money. Thou hast neither part nor lot in this matter: for thy heart is not right in the sight of God. Repent therefore of this thy wickedness, and pray God, if perhaps the thought of thine heart may be forgiven thee. For I perceive that thou art in the gall of bitterness, and in the bond of iniquity."

Simon professed salvation and desired to be great in the work of the church. When he saw the apostles' power to impart the Holy Spirit, he craved that for himself. He wanted to be used mightily by God! Who doesn't, right? Peter's admonition to all of us who desire to be great in our ministries is sobering. Peter's response was one of rage. Why? Simon did not understand Grace. God deals with His repentant children in Grace and Mercy.

Before I went to the Ranch, I was told that the gifts and calling of God are without repentance. I did not believe it. I thought I was without hope. I was convinced that God never would be able to use me again in any ministry. All I wanted was to be forgiven by my wife and have an opportunity to restore our marriage. I had absolutely no desire, zero thoughts, about ever being able to minister.

During the middle of my fifth month at the Ranch, I received a letter from a pastor who asked me to consider moving to his city, where I would become a member of the church he pastored, and, over the next two years, walk out my repentance, before beginning a ministry for sexual addicts. He wanted me to lead a ministry under the umbrella of his Baptist church. Would I consider it?

"NO! I can't even pray about such a request," was my very quick answer. At this time, I was, *myself,* in a live-in program for sexual addiction. I had no idea when I would be released. I was not looking to be in a ministry, and I certainly did *not* feel led to start a new ministry. What did I want? An opportunity to work toward reconciliation with my wife. No matter how long it would take, and no matter what I had to do, I would do it.

Two very close friends, John and Adrian, came to visit me

shortly after I had received that letter. They drove over nine hours one way to visit me. They stayed overnight, leaving at noon the next day. When I shared with them the request to prayerfully consider my starting a new ministry, they both said, "Why not?" Their time, though brief, was a tremendous encouragement. When they left they said, "You are going to be all right. You have changed. We can see it."

God was teaching me to live for Him supremely, to lean upon Him, to give up what I thought were my rights, to allow Him to occupy my thinking, to dwell in His presence daily, to pray with thanksgiving, and to live for His glory. It was more than correct doctrine. It was being intimate with my Savior, Jesus Christ. I was learning to live under authority. Most of my life, I had been the authority. There was a sense of freedom, as I submitted to God's will and to His Word.

To my surprise, two months later my counselor told me that they were considering releasing me. They called it "graduation". I was shocked. I was sure that I was going to be there for the full twelve months. Apprehension challenged my faith. We began discussing the future. "Where would I go? Did I have a place to live? What about transportation?" I had no answers.

Then John and Adrian's words, "Why not?" came to mind. Why not? I thought *I was disqualified.* Why not? *I only wanted to work toward restoring my marriage.* Why not? *I don't want to.* I called my wife and told her that I was going to graduate. I asked her if I could move to the area where she was - not to stay with her, but only to be in the same town so that we could slowly work toward restoration. I knew that there were an abundance of employment opportunities, churches, and Biblical counselors there, and I would have a place to live with a man who would be graduating a month prior to my finishing the program. Her answer was quick and simple. "If you move here, I will leave." Broken-hearted, I responded, "I will not come."

I had several discussions with my pastor about his request. I began to pray about making the move. Still, I was not sure that "the gifts and calling of God are without repentance," but I determined that *at least* I would tell God that I was "available" if He *could* use me, or if He still desired to use me.

When I graduated on April 12, 2012, I only wanted to find a good paying job, a place to live, and the opportunity to walk out my repentance. It had been my hope that I would be able to do that near my wife so that we could begin working toward reconciliation, but that door had been closed. Now my desire was to live and work "wherever" in order to prove myself by my actions, and not by my words alone.

I learned that God develops our ministries in stages.

I decided to stay in Dry Ridge, Kentucky, because I had a job, a place to live, and a good church. My pastor at Dry Ridge Baptist church was Dr. Daniel Wilson. I began attending the Wednesday following my graduation. No one goes to Dry Ridge on purpose. So the frequent question that I was asked was, "What brought you to Dry Ridge?" When pastor asked me this after my third visit, we sat down, and I told him my story. I told him about my sexual sin, my seven months at the Ranch, and how I had devastated my wife and children. I even volunteered to find another church. He assured me that I was welcome, and soon he became a counselor and friend. I joined the church on May 21. During that time, I prayed seeking the Lord's will. It is a Southern Baptist Church, and I am an independent Baptist, but he was a tremendous preacher/teacher - one of the best I have ever heard. God had already broken me, showing me many truths, and Dry Ridge Baptist became my home where I was spiritually fed. At that point, I needed what they had.

My personal life and my developing ministry began to merge.

I continued working as many hours as possible. I worked with a 19 year old former heroin addict on one side and a self-proclaimed 26 year old alcoholic on the other side of me. These men, and others, began coming to me asking about *my faith*.

I was about to take my developing ministry to the local church level.

Dr. Wilson told me of the great drug problems in Dry Ridge. He introduced me to a young man in our church who was addicted to internet pornography, and to a young woman whose husband was a deacon in our church, and yet was guilty of adultery. He asked me if I would consider teaching a six-week Wednesday night class on the subject of addictions, including: How can the church minister, and how can the church forgive? That was in May, shortly after I had become a member. He wanted the class to begin the first Wednesday in September following Labor Day.

I objected, "No, I do not believe I can do that. I am not qualified." But that did not end it.

He simply replied, "Just pray about it."

Really, at this point, I felt I could not even pray about it, but the Lord kept putting people before me who had needs. This happened at work, at church, and even when I went shopping at Wal Mart. Pastor and I were meeting on a regular basis. He would ask me if I was praying about teaching in September. He said, "You are more qualified to meet the needs of our people than you think or know. However, if you cannot do it emotionally, and if it is going to hurt you, then I do not want you to do it."

That is when I *really* began to pray and to seek the Lord's mind. He was revealing to me that I was going to have to make a choice, either to live in shame and self-pity, or to trust Him, and, through pain, be an example and a help to others.

I spoke to my former counselor. I asked him, "How can I minister? Look what I have done. Divorce is possibly in my future."

He said, "Gabe, while you were here, you learned to submit to authority. You learned to walk with the Lord, "pressing" into Him. You are under the authority of your local church and your pastor. Trust the Lord and the pastor under which he has placed you."

For the first time in my new life and ministry, I began to teach. In September, I taught a six-week course on: *God's Word: Our Guide to Psychological Issues.* I also sought out the counsel of Dr. Weniger and Pastor Mike McGee. Why? Since I had deceived myself for so long, I knew that I needed the advice of godly men who would not coddle me, but who would tell me the truth.

I sent several e-cards at Christmas, but only my friend Bob Kyner responded. He wrote back, "Call me." I sent him my phone number, thinking that if he really wants to talk to me, he will call. He did call. I admitted all of my sin to him, and we wept together.

He said, "Gabe, you have really blown it, but you are still my friend."

During this time, God burdened my heart with Jude 22, *"And of some have compassion, making a difference."* I continued to minister at my church: first, teaching the classes on addictions, then substituting for one of the adult classes. The first lesson was on *marriage!* God was reminding me that He had a sense of humor. So, I stood before the class and shared my testimony. It was more of a positive lesson from a negative act. Then, I had the opportunity to preach Wednesday nights on a regular basis when my pastor resigned. God would not allow me to sit on the sidelines. My developing ministry was accelerating.

How sad that, for a few moments of sinful pleasure, I lost my family, my influence, my position, and the many opportunities that God had opened up to me. I cannot begin to adequately describe my shame. However, I have made my decision. If God will allow me to save other men, other wives, other children from the pain, disgrace, humility, loneliness, and agony ... I will, regardless of my personal pain, call men to repentance. I will confess to those who will hear, my sin, my deception, and the destruction I have forced upon the ones I love so dearly in order that they might come to repentance.

Only God can do this. I have no position, no power, and no influence. God has been very gracious to me. He could have taken me Home, but he has crushed me, and, like the potter, He is he is trying to rebuild me. I only want His plan, His glory, and His blessing. Right now, I continue to wait upon the Lord. I trust Him, and I love him. I know that He will do that which is right.

Repentance is hard work. We are at war. We must take heed lest we fall.

Conversations with Brother Gabe

Dr. Brad Weniger: What do you say to people who pass judgment on you and, for their reasons, say that you have *not* truly repented? Is it an unforgiving spirit and an overactive imagination on their part?

Brother Gabriel Rivera: I will confess to you that this is a very painful subject for me. I have had to come to terms with what *repentance* really is. Repentance is a change of attitude, a change of direction, sincere sorrow (toward God on account of my sin), and surrendering to the will of God. My repentance is before God. No human being can know my heart. Only those who are either guilty themselves or who have been hurt so deeply in the past would dare to sit in judgment of a repentant brother or sister. I would hope that, in compassion, we would seek to restore, reconcile, and re-build.

Dr. Brad Weniger: I would think that the accusers in this case have their own problems or issues which need spiritual attention. After all, you've confessed *everything.* That's humbling enough! You were broken *that God might restore you and once again use you for His glory.* You were *not* broken so that those who did not commit the same sin could gloat about it. Do you believe that some people try to elevate themselves by consigning a designation of "permanent disqualification" to repentant sinners?

Brother Gabriel Rivera: As long as we are in this body of flesh, we will have trials. I have moved forward. My responsibility is to get close to my Savior. Obviously, I have not always made Christ my only priority. I will not sin that way again! I do believe that all of us would be wise to consider our own relationship with Christ, before judging another. Matthew 7:3, *"And why beholdest thou the mote that is in thy brother's eye, but considerest not the beam that is in thine own eye?* "Once again, *pride* is so damaging, but we do *not* see it. Think about it. Jesus Christ clearly states, do not judge. Yet, we will say to a brother or sister, "I do not believe that you have repented." Too often, we go beyond what Scripture says in order to *disqualify* a person whom God has restored.

Dr. Brad Weniger: You said, "Repentance is hard work." What did you mean?

Brother Gabriel Rivera: Once you have fallen, you carry the burden of trying to be perfect. You cannot be perfect, and, while the Lord does not expect you to be perfect, you think that you need to be perfect. You are aware that everyone is watching your every move, listening to your every word, and has an opinion on your every emotion. The truth is that you are still just a redeemed sinner. You must remember that you only need to please the Lord. I had the tendency to make people bigger than my God. Pride caused me to care too much what people thought. "How do they perceive me?" You also have Satan working to keep you from your quiet time and prayer time. Satan tempts you in your areas of past vulnerability. Satan does not want your life to glorify Christ. To stay single minded, whole hearted, and available for service requires commitment.

Dr. Brad Weniger: Do you believe God leaves any repentant child of God in a permanent "limbo" of non-service on all levels, or will he put every repentant believer into some area of service, if they're willing?

Brother Gabriel Rivera: God will use anyone who is willing to be used by Him. Of course, you must come to Him on His terms. The gifts and the calling of God *are* without repentance. I believe that with all of my heart. I have told the Lord, "I am available. Use me any way You desire."

DOUBLE-SOUL

CHAPTER 9

The Birth of Jude 22 International Ministries

Compassion: Christ is our Example

It's true. Christ meets every need. That includes our need for compassion. I desperately craved compassion when confronted with my sexual addiction, and there was little forthcoming.

Matthew 9:35-38, gives the account of Christ standing before a crowd of helpless people, who were like sheep without a shepherd to feed them, to protect them, and to guide them. He saw their need and was moved with deep sympathy.

"And Jesus went about all the cities and villages, teaching in their synagogues, and preaching the gospel of the kingdom, and healing every sickness and every disease among the people. But when he saw the multitudes, he was moved with compassion on them, because they fainted, and were scattered abroad, as sheep having no shepherd. Then saith he unto his disciples, The harvest truly is plenteous, but the laborers are few; Pray ye therefore the Lord of the harvest, that he will send forth laborers into his harvest."

Compassion ... it's the ability to see, to feel, and to identify with the miserable conditions and needs of another human being.

Here are some tough questions:

Are you a man or woman of compassion? Is your church known for its compassion? Do you seek out those who are in need? Do you have a plan to minister to the unwed mother? If she came to your church, would you invite her to sit with you? What about that homeless man whom you drive by every day on your way to work? Have you ever given him a sandwich or a cup of coffee, or did you just turn your head as you drove past? Are you aware of any teenagers without fathers in the home? Have you considered taking them to a ball game or helping them get to a Christian camp for a week or two? What about that young couple in your Sunday school class that has been absent for two months? Did you ever call them or visit their home to see if they needed some help? Rumor has it that the husband is cheating on his wife. Oh, that's right; you don't want to get involved!

The "problem" is that WE are the problem! We, who are Christians, do not want to be involved! Yet, the Bible is clear that we who are Christians are to, "Bear ye one another's burdens, and so fulfill the law of Christ," Galatians 6:2. It seems easy to excuse our lack of involvement when we're just talking with one another, but what will we say at the judgment seat of Christ? Friend, you and I need to become involved.

The cry of those in sexual sin needs to be heard and must be answered. It is not sufficient to discipline them, nor to simply pray for them. We must 'fulfil the law of Christ.' A serving Christian *HELPS*. A serving Christian is *AVAILABLE*. A serving Christian is *TOUCHED* by the infirmities of those around him. A serving Christian *EDIFIES* those who have fallen and cannot get up without a helping, caring hand extended to them.

Helps, available, touched, and edifies. These are key terms in the formula in order to fulfill the law of Christ. What is the law of Christ? In one word: *LOVE!* Galatians 5:14, *"For all the law is fulfilled in one word, even in this; Thou shalt love thy neighbor as thyself."* While you are serving, help in the time of need. Be available when it seems no one else cares. Allow your heart to be touched as Christ's heart was when he saw the multitude as sheep having no shepherd. That's when you truly feel their pain and identify with their hopelessness.

The stated purpose of Jude 22 International Ministries is to pick up, hold up, and build up fallen brothers. We bring healing to broken families by providing them with Biblical counseling and teaching resources. We offer a public speaking ministry with the goal of leading men to salvation in Jesus Christ and Christians to victory over sexual sin through an intimate relationship with Jesus Christ.

We're praying now that the Lord will provide the facilities, Biblical counselors, and staff in a place of refuge for men, who, like the prodigal son, have come to themselves and desire to confess, repent, and receive the discipline required to renew their mind. Humanly speaking, this will not be an easy task. It will call for God's people to step up to meet the challenge of fulfilling the law of Christ. It will mean pulling our head out of the sand and honestly admitting that there is widespread sexual sin in our churches. It will mean being ready to pick up a fallen brother or sister. It will mean working to hold up your father, mother, brother, sister, or friend who cannot stand alone. *(They should not stand alone!)* It will mean sacrificing your time, your money, and even your personal living space in order that you might build up that person for whom Christ died. *(You, not your neighbor. You, not your pastor. YOU!)*

No single individual can accomplish this alone. It must be done through the local church. Think with me for a moment, will you? Is this not part of the Great Commission? *"Go ye therefore, and teach all nations, **baptizing** them in the name of the Father, and of the Son, and of the Holy Ghost: **Teaching** them to observe all things whatsoever I have commanded you: and, lo, I am with you always, even unto the end of the world. Amen,"* Matthew 28:19, 20.

Go, baptize, teach, and help.

Go, baptize, teach, and be available. Go, baptize, teach and be touched. Go, baptize, teach and edify.

"Two are better than one; because they have a good reward for their labor. For if they fall, the one will lift up his fellow: but woe to him that is alone when he falleth; for he hath not another to help him up. Again, if two lie together, then they have heat: but how can one be warm alone? And if one prevail against him, two shall withstand him; and a threefold cord is not quickly broken," Ecclesiastes 4:9-12.

Here is a vivid lesson from the past which should not be ignored in the present nor in the future. We all need someone regardless of our struggle: habitual sexual sin, anger, pride, lying, gossip, or a spirit of condemnation. In every case we need someone to help us. I am thankful for the men whom God has put in my life. They have counseled me, rebuked me, corrected me, encouraged me, and have helped me find the strength that I need to obey the Lord. Pastor Brad Weniger, Pastor Mike McGee, Brother Brad Whitney, Pastor Daniel Wilson - thank you for your faithfulness. We all need someone. Will you *be* that compassionate someone in a needy person's life?

As the Lord builds Jude 22 International Ministries, it will be because of your encouragement. The need is great! Men and women need to know that there are those who will *pick* them up, *hold* them up and *build* them up for the glory of God.

Let me say, *believers must be compassionate.* Philippians 2:1-5 says, *"If there be therefore any consolation in Christ, if any **comfort of love,** if any **fellowship of the Spirit,** if any bowels and mercies, Fulfil ye my joy, that ye be likeminded, having the same love, being of one accord, of one mind. Let nothing be done through strife or vainglory; **but in lowliness of mind let each esteem other better than themselves.** Look not every man on his own things, but every man also on the things of others. Let this mind be in you, which was also in Christ Jesus."*

We are never more like Christ than when we are preferring others, serving others, finding new ways to minister mercy, and giving the greatest gift we could ever give - *the gift of love!* Colossians 3:12-14,

*"Put on therefore, as the elect of God, holy and beloved, bowels of **mercies, kindness,** humbleness of mind, meekness, longsuffering; Forbearing one another, and **forgiving one another,** if any man have a quarrel against any: even as Christ forgave you, so also do ye. And above all these things **put on charity,** which is the bond of perfectness."*

The story of the Good Samaritan in Luke 10 is one of the most familiar in the gospels. It has at least two levels of interpretation, but let's consider just one. If we're like the Samaritan, with the heart of a neighbor, we will see and help others as if they were our neighbor.

"And he said, He that showed mercy on him. Then said Jesus unto him, Go, and do thou likewise," Luke 10:37.

What are we waiting for?

Conversations with Brother Gabe

Dr. Brad Weniger: Jude 22 speaks volumes in eight words. *"And of some have compassion, making a difference."* Where would Gabe Rivera be today without compassion?

Brother Gabriel Rivera: Without a doubt, I would still be on the spiral of degradation, falling further and further from my Lord. I needed someone who loved me enough to tell me the truth about ME.

Dr. Brad Weniger: Would you say a *typical* Bible believing church could use some more compassion? Where does that *start* and *how* is that done?

Brother Gabriel Rivera: Yes, I do believe that a typical Bible believing church could use some more compassion. I served as a pastor, Christian educator, and missionary for thirty-three years. I have heard many discussions in these venues about the need for our churches to be more compassionate. It is a subject which comes up when we let our guard down. Where does it start? The only place it can start is with the Pastor. His relationship to his people, his community, and his pulpit is vital. His priorities are important as well. They need to be *clearly* defined. Does he love programs, buildings, or people? Does he love the lost? What is he personally doing to win the lost? How is this accomplished? It is accomplished by loving one person at a time, and by being sensitive to those whom God puts into your sphere of influence each day (Galatians 6:1-7; James 1:22-24; and Jude 22, 23).

Dr. Brad Weniger: Are pastors, churches, individual Christians, and families now "waking up" to their opportunities to demonstrate genuine compassion? What are you seeing?

Brother Gabriel Rivera: Yes, I believe that there are more and more pastors, churches, and individual Christians who have a sincere desire to practice Jude 22 and 23. We must be a people of action.

The world is not seeking to know Jesus Christ. We must tell them. There are people in our churches who need love and direction. It will take the sacrifice of our time if we are to be effective. I have spoken with a number of pastors who agree that there is a huge need in our churches today for a ministry such as Jude 22. They just don't know exactly how to implement such a ministry. That is what I am being told by many pastors. They know that sexual sin is an epidemic in our churches. Because of these conversations, there is hope that we *can* and that we will rescue those in bondage.

Dr. Brad Weniger: What is the primary fear which holds back some who might demonstrate compassion? Do they think if they forgive or if they show compassion they might "get burned"?

Brother Gabriel Rivera: I am not sure if it is fear or if it is just failure to practice compassion consistently. Because we did not want to be labeled "preachers of the social gospel," we stayed clear of social issues. While I agree that we should never compromise the preaching of the Gospel, we *should* take a hard look at the ministry of Christ. I do believe there is a fear of "getting burned" by many, and I know this is a distinct possibility. However, fear should not dictate my obedience to the Scripture.

Dr. Brad Weniger: Is it worth "the risk" to show compassion?

Brother Gabriel Rivera: Yes, yes, yes! D.L. Moody said, *"There, but for the Grace of God, go I."* We never know what God has planned for any soul. A double-souled individual, a sex addict, or a homeless individual each can be transformed by our loving God. God only gets the opportunity when we, his children, risk going into the house that is on fire in order to bring them out!

CHAPTER 10

What is Sexual Addiction?

Don't panic. I am not going to graphically define sexual addiction. Actually, I have found that it is almost impossible to come to *any* definitive conclusion concerning the use of the word "addiction". I am going to merely share with you what works for me and what I believe will be a help to you.

There is no question that our American culture has been influenced by fanciful theories when it comes to psychotherapy. Just glance at the ever expanding *Diagnostic and Statistical Manual of Mental Disorders,* and you'll discover that we have a compulsion to create a new term for any unexplainable behavior.

During my research, I found that many in the field of psychology cannot agree concerning the authenticity of sexual addiction. One definition suggests an inability to overcome:

Being given over to an undesirable habit to the point of dependence. Psychologists make a distinction between psychological and physical addiction.

To some, the use of the word *addiction* implies that I have no responsibility. In other words, I am simply ill, so, please, excuse my behavior. However, in addition to being wrong, it takes away my hope. So instead of using the term "addiction", let us use *slavery*. If I am not able to free myself from something, am I not then a slave? If I am a slave, who then is my master? Whom do I worship?

"Jesus answered them, Verily, verily, I say unto you, whosoever committeth sin is the servant of sin," (John 8:34).

In the rudimentary beginnings, I believe that I am in control. I seek after that which gratifies my flesh. However, *as I follow this path,* I find that I am really worshipping *myself.* Because I am worshipping *myself,* I indulge in my appetites. Overtime, I find that I am habitually indulging and that I have become a slave. Therefore, what I am really doing is engaging in *idolatry.*

So, what is idolatry? Idolatry is an act of worship to an image or a created being. Idolatry includes covetousness, self-indulgence, pride, and it is irrational. (I know all of these experientially!) We do not like to use this term, 'idolatry', but the Scriptures cannot lie. Please, do not take my word alone on this. Search the Scriptures, Deuteronomy 5:8, 9; 8:19; Joshua 23:6-8; Ephesians 5:5; Philippians 3:18, 19; Ezekiel 28:2; and Isaiah 44:10-20.

Friend, if you are involved in sexual sin on any level, you need to know that you are dealing with idols. Anything that we love more than Jesus Christ is an idol. You do not have a mental illness. You do not have a disease. Your problem is SIN. Your problem is your perspective of God. God views sexual addiction as sin. Do you?

In his book, *ADDICTIONS, A Banquet in the Grave,* Dr. Edward T. Welch points out the difference between a disease and an addiction.

When we have a disease, we can still be growing in the knowledge of Christ, but addictions are incompatible with spiritual growth.

There it is - your only hope is to have your sin exposed and then be led to repentance. Your will must be broken. You must renew your mind concerning your sin and develop a Biblical view of God. In essence, you need to see your sin as God sees it. Apart from the power of God, you will remain in a state of hopelessness. I can testify to the love and changing power of a holy God Who never, ever gave up on me. Friends walked away. Family rejected the work of God in my life. But God said, *"Let your conversation be without covetousness; and be content with such things as ye have: for he hath said,*

I will never leave thee, nor forsake thee," Hebrews 13:5. In other words, "I am all you need." Think about that! I certainly have. After twenty-seven years of my disobedience, Jesus Christ still came after me and would not let me go. Christ has shown me that when people are big, God is small.

What are you going to believe? Will you believe the humanistic definition which says that you have a disease, or will you believe the Word of God? The choice is clear. If you want to be set free, you must reconstruct every area of your life. Your manner of life, your self-control, and your thinking all need to come under the control of the Holy Spirit. This will take time. You will need help. By the grace of God, Jude 22 International Ministries will be here to help you!

A person who is in bondage to sexual sin will also face cruel and unfair accusations. When I was at the Ranch, cars would drive by, and the occupant would scream out obscenities. "Pervert! Child molester! (And more)." However, the cruelest accusations for me were not those drive by curses, but were from my own family members! About a week before Christmas, I received a phone call during which I was falsely accused of child molestation. This was without any evidence whatsoever, and it caught me off-guard when I was most vulnerable. I have repeatedly offered to take a lie detector test. This lie came "out of left field." That is the way Satan does his worst damage.

Not every person who is a slave to sexual sin is a predator, a child molester, or a pedophile. These are all serious crimes. Even the church does not always know the legal or moral differences regarding such acts. I am not now, nor have I ever been, a predator, a child molester, or a pedophile. Yet, research shows that it is a common *accusation* against those involved in sexual sin. Sad.

I will now share some simple truths which are available to anyone who may be willing to invest time in research.

What is a Predator?
A sexual predator is defined as a person who is an adult or juvenile who has been convicted of, or pleaded guilty to, committing

a sexually oriented offense and who is likely in the future to commit additional sexually oriented offenses. U.S. Legal.com.

What is a Child Molester?
Child sexual abuse or child molestation is a form of child abuse in which an adult or older adolescent uses a child for sexual stimulation. "Child Sexual Abuse". Medline Plus. U.S. National Library of Medicine, 2008-04-02.

What is a Pedophile?
A pedophile is a person 16 years of age or older who is primarily or exclusively sexually attracted to children who have not begun puberty (girls 10 years old or less, and boys 11 year old or less, on average). The prepubescent child must be at least five years younger than the person in the case of adolescent pedophiles before the attraction can be diagnosed as pedophilia. DIAGNOSTIC CRITERIA FOR PEDOPHILIA" (PDF). APA STATEMENT. American Psychiatric Association. June 17, 2003.

A person who has committed any of the above acts and has been arrested is considered a **sex offender.** *A sex offender is a generic term for all persons convicted of crimes involving sex, including rape, molestation, sexual harassment and pornography production or distribution. In most states convicted sex offenders are supposed to report to local police authorities, but many do not.* U.S. Legal.com

We live in a world that is not our home. We are strangers and pilgrims.

We are looking for the coming of Jesus Christ. However, while we wait, we need to be vigilant in our soul-winning and in our ministry to those in bondage.

According to the pastors who have spoken to me, I conclude that we are facing an epidemic of sexual sin in our churches. The pulpit, the pew, the Christian School classroom, and the mission field ALL are *at risk.* Consider the following statistics from internet filter provider *Covenant Eyes:*

Porn in the Church

Pornography is prevalent everywhere today. In fact, 1 in 8 online searches is for pornography.

Because porn use thrives in secrecy, many church members are trapped in a cycle of sin and shame, thinking that they're the only ones facing this temptation.

70% of American men ages 18-34 view Internet pornography once a month.

"For nothing is secret, that shall not be made manifest; neither anything hid, that shall not be known and come abroad.

It is Epidemic

Regular church attendees are 26% less likely to look at porn than non-attendees, but those self-identified as "fundamentalists" are 91% more likely to look at porn.

50% of Christian men are addicted to pornography.

37% of pastors admit that cyber-porn is a current struggle and 51% believe it is a source of temptation. (I would think this would be 100%)

47% of families said pornography is a problem in their home.
This is Porn in the Church! I was a statistic!!

Did you know...?

9 out of 10 boys were exposed to pornography before the age of 18. 6 out of 10 girls were exposed to pornography before the age of 18. 71% of teens hide online behavior from their parents.

"Because that, when they knew God, they glorified him not as God, neither were thankful; but became vain in their imaginations, and their foolish heart was darkened. Professing themselves to be wise, they became fools," Romans 1:21, 22.

What are you prepared to do? While this book is dealing with my personal sexual sin, disobedience, and loss, what about you? Do realize that there could be many influences and activities in your life which could control and eventually destroy you? For example, substance abuse, overeating, shopping, exercise, gambling, work, sex/pornography, internet/TV/movies, sports, and lying are just a few of the ways Satan can come between you and your God. When he does, it is called IDOLATRY.

Conversations with Brother Gabe

Dr. Brad Weniger: Thank you for speaking *plainly,* yet *appropriately,* on the subject of sexual addiction. I don't recall ever hearing a message or attending a seminar on that subject in any church in the last six decades! How common was sexual addiction in the churches in the last century, and why the silence for so long?

Brother Gabriel Rivera: Perhaps it was a fear of being inappropriate, or perhaps it was a lack of sensitivity, but little was ever preached on the subject of sexual addiction in the past. There were plenty of sex offenders and sexual sins, but very little *was plainly* said. For example, in 1948 Dr. Alfred Kinsey, a biologist, wrote *Sexual Behavior in the Human Male.* He interviewed 1,400 convicted sex offenders. Later, he turned his attention to questioning prostitutes, and he wrote *Sexual Behavior in the Human Female* in 1953. Society excitedly accepted his false assertion that nearly everyone had succumbed to an affair. He also postulated the belief that most people had actually engaged in perverted sex, including homosexuality and bestiality! Kinsey's conclusion were popularized in 1954, when Playboy hit the newsstands. In the 1970's, the Feminist movement began to grow in power and influence. One result was *the sexual revolution* during the last half of the twentieth century. The church struggled to establish a viable position, teaching, and defense for the aggressive attacks from the sexual revolution. Teens especially needed more than "just flee fornication." The typical Sunday school curriculum failed to boldly teach what the Scripture says concerning human sexuality.

Dr. Brad Weniger: A Christian friend of mine, who is intelligent and well-read, has questioned the reality of sexual *addiction.* He wonders if it's nothing more than *irresponsible behavior.* What would you say to my friend in order to help him to understand the truly addictive nature of your twenty-seven year struggle?

Brother Gabriel Rivera: I understand your friend's position. Much debate has focused on the reality of *sexual addiction.* The word *addiction,* implies a lack of responsibility, but that is not what I am saying. I use the word *addiction,* because it is the best word that we have. A sexual addict experiences the same type of uncontrollable compulsions which others feel in different forms of addiction (like substance, alcohol, gambling, shopping, etc.). Addicts feel as if they are out of control. They feel like they are in bondage. Sex addicts struggle to control or to postpone sexual feelings and actions. Most sex addicts do not know how to achieve genuine intimacy, sadly forming no attachment to their sexual partners. I tried everything I thought I could. I felt hopeless. Mine that was a life that otherwise controlled, positive, and disciplined, and yet I could not break free from my sexual addiction.

Dr. Brad Weniger: Not everyone who is guilty of sexual misconduct or sexual sin is automatically a sexual *addict.* Isn't that correct?

Brother Gabriel Rivera: That is correct. One should not assume that he is a sex addict because he fantasizes about sex a lot. However, if your day to day functioning is seriously affected by something sexual, this may be an indication of a problem.

Dr. Brad Weniger: All those who have committed sexual sin need to confess it and forsake it, right?

Brother Gabriel Rivera: Proverbs 28:13, teaches us, *"He that covereth his sins shall not prosper: but whoso confesseth and forsaketh them shall have mercy."* There are no secrets with God. When we try to hide our sins from God and others, we deceive ourselves. Hiding sin brings us destruction. We can never have peace. God only shows Mercy to those who repent and forsake their sin. Confessing sin brings us God's Mercy and forgiveness.

Dr. Brad Weniger: Practically every week we hear about preachers falling into sexual sins. It's an epidemic! Do you think that the Devil *targets* preachers and other key leaders with extraordinary sexual temptation?

Brother Gabriel Rivera: I absolutely believe that Satan targets preachers and other key leaders. Revelation 12:10 states, *"And*

I heard a loud voice saying in heaven, Now is come salvation, and strength, and the kingdom of our God, and the power of his Christ: for the accuser of our brethren is cast down, which accused them before our God day and night." Satan knows that if he can take down the leadership of a local assembly that assembly will fail. Satan attacked Job, and, in Luke 22:31, he requested permission to sift Peter like wheat.

Dr. Brad Weniger: You've spoken with many pastors and other Christian leaders. The attack of sexual temptation is relentless. Give us some suggestions on how to stand against the Devil on this and how to help those preachers and lay leaders who are under siege.

Brother Gabriel Rivera: There is no greater counsel than the Word of God. However, I discovered that my thinking was not correct. Dr. Edward Welch in his book, *Addictions A Banquet in the Grave,* said it this way, *"We don't believe what we believe."* What did he mean? It is possible to have an advanced seminary degree, to have years of ministry experience, and still fall if you do not have a practical theology, one that you *use* every day! *Stay away* from temptation. We should pray that we will not be led into temptation. *Protect* yourself against evil men and women. Proverbs 6:20, 21, *"My son, keep thy father's commandment, and forsake not the law of thy mother: Bind them continually upon thine heart, and tie them about thy neck." Walk in the Spirit!* Galatians 5:16, 17. *Squeeze* the life out of your sin. Don't let your sin live, Colossians 3: 5-7. You are going to be tempted. Do not play with temptation - *RUN!*

Dr. Brad Weniger: Someone has asked why we should receive *you* into fellowship and service for God, when other preachers whom we *know* have also committed sexual sins, but have tried to *cover* them without true repentance, have not been so received. How do you answer them?

Brother Gabriel Rivera: I believe the answer is in your question. I have confessed, repented, and submitted myself to a live-in program for my sexual addiction. I deserve hell (as we *all* do). It's never been an "easy fix", since the earthly consequences go on and on and on. However, repentance is the answer. The blood of Jesus

Christ cleanses from *all* sin. As far as God is concerned, he doesn't remember those sins anymore *and neither should we!* Why those *unrepentant* preachers persist in trying to cover their own sins instead of letting Christ's blood wash those away is beyond me! Until they do, we dare not give them "a pass." No man can have two masters! Like the prodigal son, you must eventually come to yourself.

DOUBLE-SOUL

CHAPTER 11

A Storm Now and Then

Three years have passed since that pivotal day when my wife confronted me with the truth concerning my use of internet pornography. I have travelled many roads, listened to multiple counselors, and searched the Scriptures to find the reason for the madness of my past. The reasons are clear and consistent. I followed the lust of my flesh. I was a prisoner of *double-soul-ness*. Galatians 5:17 is clear, *"This I say then, Walk in the Spirit, and ye shall not fulfill the lust of the flesh."* My life, though spiritually successful at times, was lacking a discipline that only comes through intimacy with Jesus Christ.

The Holy Spirit has torn my life apart in order that we (Christ and I) might have the relationship which I said I wanted to have forty-seven years ago. However, I was unwilling to give up total control in order to possess it. God has been faithful! He continues to teach me, reminding me that He must be Lord of all, or He is not Lord at all. My timing is not the Lord's timing. I do not always understand what He is doing. When I think that I know what to do, He often reveals to me that I do not know *anything*. Through my daily devotions, a song, a word from a friend, or a sermon at church, He clearly speaks to me, telling me that I am to wait upon Him. I want to share with you in these last chapters what my God has done. I want you to see Him and what He will do for you.

I was unemployed for eleven months. I had diligently submitted resumes, had followed up leads from friends, but no door opened. On

Easter, my pastor asked the church to give a love offering for Jude 22 International Ministries and me. Their response was overwhelming. Nearly $3500 was given. We are not a large church, but when it comes to compassion for others, there is no larger church. As the months went by, individuals would come up to me, shake my hand, and leave behind a $20, a $50, or a $100 dollar bill … always reassuring me that they were praying for me.

Because I live about fifty miles from the church, I was only able to attend Sunday mornings and Wednesday nights. Recently, various individuals or families invited me to have lunch with them enabling me to stay for the evening service. Some have taken me into their homes. The lyrics of the song *A Storm Now and Then* seem to be the perfect description of my life. This song has become very meaningful to me.

> *All my dreams were shattered and all that mattered was gone on the winds of sorrow.*
> *Everything I had planned swept out of my hand and I saw no hope for tomorrow.*
> *With my heart near to breaking, I cried, "Lord, I can't make it by myself. I just can't carry on."*
> *And with the storm at its darkest came His words, "I'll never leave you. You are loved. Let my Strength be your own.*
> *Chorus*
> *It takes a storm now and then to remind me to depend to depend on the Lord And to rest in His word.*
> *For in the wind and the rain, I learned to call on His name And I thank Him in my song   It took a storm to make me strong. When my feet are stumbling and my hopes are crumbling*
> *The Lord is there guiding He is peace. He is calm in the midst of the storm the Lord is there abiding*
> *He is grace. He is power. He is strength for each hour. He is comfort and safety from all harm.*
> *There is joy in my soul for the Lord has control and beneath are His everlasting arms" (by the Booth Brothers)*

God knows our struggles. We are never, ever alone. It is important to grasp this truth, because Satan is very clever in getting us to think that we are *alone*. Have you ever questioned or wondered how the devil is so successful? Of course, he has had millenniums of experience since he was created an archangel with beauty and wisdom. However, I believe his *greater success* comes when we put more confidence in the people around us than we put in Jesus Christ. All of us suffer from a degree of peer (people) pressure. We want to please our spouse, our children, our co-workers, our friends, our pastor, our boss, our neighbors, and our God. The list is really endless. Ask yourself this question, "Where do I put Jesus Christ on my list?" I know what we *say,* but I am more interested in what we *do.*

Think about this. It takes a storm now and then to remind me to depend on the Lord and to rest in His Word. I do not know about you, but, for me, God had to shatter my dreams. All of my plans vanished, and I was left with nothing but a feeling of hopelessness. It was only as I realized that God was loving me through my storm and that he had a plan for my life, that I stopped caring about the opinions of my spouse, my children, my co-workers, my friends, and even my own opinions. I only wanted to know what God said, and I only wanted to follow where He was leading. It has not been easy. My flesh still wants to be in control. Only by dying daily, often many times during the day, can you be victorious. I have a godly pastor and a great church standing with me. When the devil is pounding at my door and I really do want to quit, they pick me up. As I endeavor to put God first in everything that I do, He supplies my needs. Every physical, emotional, and spiritual need is supplied. When my feet are stumbling and my hopes are crumbling, He uses His church to hold me up.

Friend, God's Grace and Mercy, as well as His power and strength, are available to every sinner who will repent. He will never leave you nor forsake you. He will give you the courage to stand. You're not alone, for He will be by your side.

At the time of this writing, I am sixty years old. I have always been considered a leader, the person who you want on your team, and the one who will get the job done. That may sound good. However, Satan used these characteristics to deftly plant seeds of pride. For three years, God in His Mercy has been uprooting those seeds of pride which caused so much destruction. The Lord has been teaching me that this is *His* team and *He* is the leader. I must follow and obey.

Being unemployed has forced me to let go and let God. In the past, no matter how bad things were, I used to boast, "Well, I have never had anything repossessed!" Right now I am months behind in my car payment. I have no way to pay my bills. I am a diabetic. I have been without medication for months. Now hear this! If my God is in control, and He is, then I have *nothing* to be concerned about. What do I mean? Am I being slothful? Am I being irresponsible? NO! I am trusting God. I am applying His Word. I am standing on His Precious Promises. He knows that I have a car payment. He knows that I have bills. He knows that I am a diabetic. Will He *not* supply according to His riches in glory by Christ Jesus?

You see, just like you, I also have days when I need to be reminded of my God's Love. Satan desires to sift us like wheat by lying to us and by making our needs seem too large for God to meet. I confess that I need my pastor, my church, my godly friends, and my family to be patient with me while God is reconstructing my life. This reconstruction means: a new manner of life, a renewed mind, a teachable spirit, and walk that is by faith and not by sight.

What has God done? He provided an opportunity to umpire baseball games and referee volleyball matches. This opportunity temporarily met my needs for several months. He gave me a speaking opportunity where the honorarium was enough to pay a bill. Through three individuals on one Sunday, God put $320.00 in my hand. The next day, my pastor called to let me know that there was a total of $354.00 given in the offering for me. In one day, $674.00! I wept. No matter what Satan was throwing my way, my God was standing in front of me, deflecting and providing for me.

I am very grateful for my younger daughter and her husband. When I became unemployed and had no place to live, they invited me to stay with them. I realize the great sacrifice which they are making on my behalf. It is not easy. First, my daughter is also still healing from the revelation of my double-life. She cares for three young children and her husband, and as a pastor's wife, she has a ministry to her church. Because I had no other place to go, I accepted their offer, thinking it would only be for a couple of months. As I sit in what was supposed to be my granddaughter's room, my stay extended beyond nine months! I know that my presence could be an inconvenience for them, as it would be for any family. With three children ages 5, 2 and 1, there is always something that needs to be done. While I am blessed to be able to see my grandchildren every day, I still struggle with the burden of not being able to contribute financially. This is just another example of God saying, "Wait. Your timing is not my timing." It is a *humbling* experience.

God knows that He needs to keep me humble and broken. The pain of my sin must be greater than the fleeting pleasure of my sin. He wants me to remember that my sin was first against Him. Our God is a jealous God, and He will not allow His children to worship idols. These truths have become primary to my sustained growth. In order to be intimate with Christ, I must never forget who He is, what He has done, and I must remember that He has forgiven me of my sin and has restored me.

Conversations with Brother Gabe

Dr. Brad Weniger: You speak of "intimacy with Christ." What does that mean? Break it down into practical *steps* for us.

Brother Gabriel Rivera: To me, intimacy means to be familiar or personal. We need to know more than just the names of Christ. We need to know Abba Father! We need to be consumed with the being of Jesus Christ. Understand that we need Him just as much as we need the air we breathe. For me, that means seeking Him early. Before I get out of bed in the morning, I am speaking with my Lord. I'm reading the Bible *for me,* (not for others) and I'm taking the time to really study His Word. Scripture memorization is important. How can I fight the Devil if I have no ammunition? My words have no power, but God's Word is *all powerful!* I'm learning to live in His presence and to be conscious of Him throughout the whole day, not just in my morning quiet time. We should think of others that we might be a blessing to them. By these exercises we are drawn closer to Christ. We can have His mind, not our own.

Dr. Brad Weniger: The *Lordship* of Christ doesn't mean *salvation.* While acknowledging Christ as Lord is *ideal,* it is not always a reality. What is the greatest need in order for us to experience the Lordship of Christ? What do we need to *do?*

Brother Gabriel Rivera: We must be willing to let go of our life and let Christ have control. Pride is the enemy of my soul, (and it is your enemy as well). We must learn to trust His Word rather than our feelings. We must understand that when He says *WAIT,* He means for us to stop going where we *think* we should go, and just *WAIT!* This has been most difficult for me. I have always been one to go, go, and go. So many times in the last three years, God has clearly told me to *WAIT.* I have not always understood, but I have obeyed, even when well-meaning friends thought that I should go. To make Christ Lord means allowing Him to lead. "Speak, Lord, for your servant heareth!"

Dr. Brad Weniger: Do you see a lot of Christians, even leaders, appearing to place more confidence in those around them than in the Lord Jesus Christ? Since you confessed to being guilty of this yourself, are you now more aware of this in others?

Brother Gabriel Rivera: I cannot judge anyone else, but it would *appear* to be that way. Pastors and their congregations need to look long and hard at the mess that misplaced confidence caused in *my* life and ministry and then be warned!

Dr. Brad Weniger: You've had some part-time employment (to keep body and soul together), but no full-time job. That's got to be *rough* on your ego. You *want* to work and to contribute financially, but doors which ought to open, seem to slam shut. What is God saying to you and to others?

Brother Gabriel Rivera: With every closed door, God is saying to me, "Gabe, I want you to stay humble and broken. *Trust Me!*"

Trust and obey for there is no other way! I confess to you that only recently have I really come to grips with this truth. God knows that I have a car payment. God knows that I need insurance. God knows that I have diabetes, and that I need my medication. He will give me what He wants me to have at the exact time that He wants me to have it. This is not always comfortable. Sometimes I am left wondering, "When Lord?" He has broken and humbled me for His purpose. I must wait upon Him to fulfill that purpose *in His time*. I really believe that He has kept me unemployed in order to write this book and to establish a worldwide ministry - Jude 22 International Ministries - which is in the developmental stages. God has a purpose, and I am not going to sacrifice the eternal on the altar of the immediate.

Dr. Brad Weniger: It would be a tragedy to abandon the long, uphill climb to God's perfect will when you're just ten feet from the top.

Brother Gabriel Rivera: The hill has been much steeper than I ever imagined when I first began, but I am not complaining. God has given me peace. I know that I'm doing what I am because He wants me to stand in the gap. More preachers than we can count have fallen before me. I could have done what so many of them have done - *Nothing!* And I was very willing to do just that, but God kept seeking me out and offering me opportunities to share my story. It is painful. It is exceedingly difficult! However, if one man, or one family can be rescued, it will be worth all of the pain. Paul said, *"Not that I speak in respect of want: for I have learned, in whatsoever state I am, therewith to be content."* It is not about me.

Dr. Brad Weniger: Thank God for His *sustaining* Grace! We *can* be content.

Brother Gabriel Rivera: AMEN!

DOUBLE-SOUL

CHAPTER 12

Let the Healing Begin

If you have confessed your sin to God and to those affected by your sin, you have taken the first step toward healing. Healing will not come quickly.

Just as recovery from major surgery requires time, so will your healing. Undoubtedly your confession has shocked family and friends. You may feel better, but those around you have never felt *worse!* In fact, all they are feeling right now is anger, betrayal, confusion and indescribable pain.

You want and need to be forgiven. Yes, Matthew 6:12-15, teaches us that we **must** forgive.

"And forgive us our debts, as we forgive our debtors. And lead us not into temptation, but deliver us from evil; For thine is the kingdom, and the power, and the glory, for ever. Amen. For if ye forgive men their trespasses, your heavenly Father will also forgive you: But if ye forgive not men their trespasses, neither will your Father forgive your trespasses."

However, BE PATIENT. You are not responsible whether or not others forgive you. You are responsible to confess and repent. Forgiveness is offered because I have been forgiven by Jesus Christ. Forgiveness is offered over and over and over. Why? This is how Christ forgives. The forgiveness that you should seek is from your heavenly Father. You must be sure that you are in a right relationship with Jesus Christ.

You are responsible to walk out your repentance before God. The second step in the healing process is *repentance*. The message of Jesus Christ was, and is, "repent." "From that time Jesus began to preach, and to say, *Repent: for the kingdom of heaven is at hand.*" Matthew 4:17, and *"Remember therefore from whence thou art fallen, and repent, and do the first works,"* Revelation 2:5a. In the story of the prodigal son you can see the characteristics of repentance.

- Conviction of sin – grief over offending God
- Confession of sin to God and others affected by the sin
- Desire to make restitution
- Turn from the sin (begin to put off sinful manner of life)
- Pursue godliness (begin to put on godly habits)

Acts 5:30, 31 shows that repentance is a gift from God. *"The God of our fathers raised up Jesus, whom ye slew and hanged on a tree. Him hath God exalted with his right had to be a Prince and a Saviour. For to **give repentance** to Israel, and forgiveness of sins."*

Have you turned from your sin? Have you begun to put off the sinful habits that have long enslaved you? Are you pursuing godliness by putting on godly habits daily? True repentance is among the greatest gifts given to us. It is provided by Jesus' work on the cross for our sins. Do not waste the gift that God has given you! Confession is only the beginning. Now you must strive to live a life before the world that manifests the inward work of God that He might be glorified. His glory, not your comfort, is the goal.

The healing process also includes a renewing of your mind. This comes through trust in the Lord, repentance, and meditation on God's Word. You need a Biblical change … not just counseling once a week and a new job! There must be a personal application of Bible truth. You need to change the way you think. Romans 12:1, 2, *"I beseech you therefore, brethren, by the mercies of God, that ye present your bodies a living sacrifice, holy, acceptable unto God, which is your reasonable service. And be not conformed to this world: but be ye transformed by the renewing of your mind, that ye may prove what is that good, and acceptable, and perfect, will of God."* The renewing of your mind is really an act of worship. As your mind is transformed, you will become more like Christ. You will find yourself desiring God's will and not your own. You will find peace with God, man, and yourself.

Of course, confession, repentance, and the renewing of your mind will never occur without the conviction of the Holy Spirit, revealing that you have sinned against God.

"And when he is come, he will reprove the world of sin, and of righteousness, and of judgment," John 16:8

The New Unger's Bible Dictionary offers this definition of conviction:

"The meaning of conviction as a law term is being found guilty. In common language it means being persuaded or convinced. In theology it means being condemned at the bar of one's own conscience as a sinner in view of the law of God. It is the antecedent to repentance and is often accompanied by a painful sense of exposure to God's wrath. It is the work of the Holy Spirit, showing the heinousness of sin and the soul's exposure to divine wrath. The means of conviction are various: gospel truth, the law read or heard, reflection, affliction, calamity, etc. It often comes suddenly, and may be stifled, as it surely is if not heeded."

Do you understand that you can resist the convicting power of God? Do you further grasp that if you do resist that affliction, calamity and divine wrath may knock at your door? It is conceivable that you will slowly become more immune to the pain of your sin.

As I did, so you must hear and answer His voice while you can hear it. *Double-soul-ness* will lead you to destruction.

God knocked on my door for twenty-seven years. I was blind, deaf, self- deluded, and full of pride. I saw how the Lord was blessing my family and my ministry, and I slowly lost the ability to feel the pain that accompanied my sin. I beg you today, please let the healing begin. It begins with you! Your conviction, your confession, your repentance, and the renewing of your mind are all up to you. Only then, will your family, friends, and those affected begin to heal. A song writer has put this truth into these words:

No time like the present, no place like right here, No other can cleanse you from sin;
If you came here in need of a touch from the Lord, Then let the healing begin.
Let it begin, let it begin. (Bill and Gloria Gaither)

Yes, only the Lord Jesus Christ can set you free from the bondage that has enslaved you. You will never be the husband, father, brother, or friend that God intends you to be until you kneel at the cross and make Jesus Christ your Lord. Either the healing begins with your receiving Christ as your Personal Savior, or by yielding your complete being to His will. Romans 6:16 is very clear, *"Know ye not, that to whom ye yield yourselves servants to obey, his servants ye are to whom ye obey; whether of sin unto death, or of obedience unto righteousness?"*

"Know ye not?" Paul asks. In other words, "Don't you get it?"

Most people trapped in sexual sin, or in any addiction, for that matter, do not get it. It is always right there before you. To whomever you yield yourself as a servant to obey, you are then their servants. You cannot serve two masters. Romans 8:6 declares, *"For to be carnally minded is death; but to be spiritually minded is life and peace."*

As I have traveled the path of conviction, confession, repentance, and renewing of my mind, I have learned just how very much I need to surrender daily to the Lord Jesus Christ. I lived for so long believing the lie that I only had a besetting sin, that now I will not risk leaving my room without first fellowshipping with my Lord. Every hour of every day is a battle. Satan wants to keep people from coming to saving faith in Jesus Christ, and He wants to debilitate all those who already know Christ as Savior. Satan does not want you living in the power and victory of Christ - He will do *anything,* anything, to overwhelm you and to stop you from serving the Lord. DO NOT LET IT HAPPEN! Know your MASTER! Keep in close, intimate fellowship with Him.

As I finish this book, there is nothing more in this world that I desire than to be reconciled with my wife and my children. I wish that I could tell you that we have experienced full restoration, but I cannot. My prayer is that one day the healing that I have experienced by the hand of a gracious, merciful and loving God will be accepted by them as truth. My prayer is that one day you will experience full restoration as well.

Until then, remember that you may choose your sin, but you cannot choose the consequences. May God in His mercy make the words of this song true for you and your family.

Let the healing begin
We're all here together in one accord, Brother and sisters and friends;
We came here in need of a touch from the Lord, So let the healing begin.

Conversations with Brother Gabe

Dr. Brad Weniger: You've begun to heal. That's *good!* Is every day a good day, Brother Gabe?

Brother Gabriel Rivera: Every day *is* a good day in the sense that the Lord made it, and He gives us fresh opportunities to heal, to grow, and to glorify Him. Philippians 4:13 states, *"I can do all things through Christ which strengtheneth me."* This can only be true in my life, or any Christians life, if I die daily to self. For Christ to strengthen me, I must first confess my weakness. I must know His will and be determined to fulfill His will at any cost. If I do these things, then Christ will empower me to glorify Him. That is all I want.

Dr. Brad Weniger: You can't go back and *change* anything, can you?

Brother Gabriel Rivera: No, the past is done. It's forgiven, and it's under the Blood! I revisit the past only briefly to learn, and by God's marvelous Grace, I move on. I have told the Lord that I am available if He wants to use me. My desire is to serve the Lord and to be a blessing.

Dr. Brad Weniger: Let's talk about forgiveness. You don't *deserve* it, do you?

Brother Gabriel Rivera: No, I don't deserve it, and I don't expect it on that basis. The middle part of forgiveness is the little word "give". Forgiveness is a *gift* we give. God forgives. People are slow to forgive themselves and others. We must be patient. God began teaching me about forgiveness, patience, and the fear of the Lord on December 1, 2012. While reading Psalm 130, I saw that God does not mark our iniquities. If He did, none of us could stand. God also convicted me about being *patient* and having a *fear* of the Lord. Right then and there, I vowed that no matter what came my way, I would wait on the Lord. Psalm 130 is a part of my signature.

Dr. Brad Weniger: Ugly things have been said *about* you. Ugly things have been said *to* you. What do you say to that?

Brother Gabriel Rivera: My sin *was* ugly. The hurt that I caused was *ugly*. I *deserve* ugly words and treatment. However, God has forgiven me, and that's enough. It would be better for those who have not yet forgiven to go ahead and forgive me if only *for the sake of their own spiritual healing.* I would want that *for them.* I want them to see that while my sin caused them pain, they continue to experience *a greater pain* by not forgiving. They are responsible for where they are now in their journey. No one can be blessed without forgiving others.

Dr. Brad Weniger: You say that you got to the point where you were beginning to feel "no pain" for your sin. How close do you believe you were to destruction? Did you ever think about "the sin unto death"?

Brother Gabriel Rivera: I believe that it is only the Grace of God that I am alive today. As I look back, I see multiple opportunities for repentance. I did not always see those opportunities at the time. God could have taken me out of this world many times. Actually, I prayed that He would take me Home, because I knew that I was sinning against Him. I was miserable! I love my wife, my children, and *serving the Lord.* You see, that was the problem. I loved serving, but Christ was not my *first* love. Christ loved me enough to break me, humble me, and show me myself.

Dr. Brad Weniger: Your ultimate exposure as an internet pornography user was a blessing in disguise, wasn't it? Had it not occurred, you might not be with us today, serving God and trying to save others by the Grace of God.

Brother Gabriel Rivera: That is correct. This is why I am single-minded concerning Jude 22 International Ministries. God did not leave me here to work some secular job and sit in a pew. I can do that. I would do that, if that is what He wants. I think it is clear, at least to me, that God wants to *make a difference* through me.

DOUBLE-SOUL

CHAPTER 13

One Final Thought

Years ago, my wife and I had the joy and privilege of visiting the country of Romania. At that time, Communism was very much alive and well. We met people who, under tremendous persecution, flocked to the churches to hear the Word of God. Often, I would be asked by Americans, "What is the church like in Romania?" My reply was simple: "Pure and powerful!" As much as possible, they lived out the Scriptures, dealt with sin, (by exercising church discipline), and called people to live separated lives. Yes, even then, I knew that the key to God's power was to be pure in spirit. I feared that God would one day discipline me. I just thought that I could beat this thing called sexual sin all alone. I was wrong. Why? I was wrong because I did not make Jesus Christ Lord of my life.

Regardless who you are - pastor, evangelist, missionary, or Christian educator – you will fall if Christ is not the Lord of your life.

If I could speak to you face to face, I would urge you to receive Jesus Christ as your *Personal* Savior and Lord. (The emphasis is on *personal.)* In our religious world today, even among fundamentalists and evangelicals, there may be many who seek to gain heaven apart from a relationship with Jesus Christ. Not only are our churches nearly empty, but there also seems to be a lack of Holy Spirit power. The waters of baptism are not stirred, the challenge of missions is ever increasing, while the response wanes. Has our God ceased to call workers into His vineyard? I think not. What then is the issue?

The only plausible answer is that we have forfeited our purity and power upon the altar of convenience. *Soul winning?* Is it ever convenient? *Discipleship?* Do you have an hour or two a week to share your life with a young convert? *Prayer Meeting?* How long does your church pray corporately in a week? Years ago on a Wednesday night, I made the statement to my congregation, "That if the only thing we do tonight is pray, it would be time well spent." An elderly man frowned at me, shook his head in disagreement, and left. *Teaching ministries?* Opportunities abound in every church. We quote the Great Commission,

> *"Go ye therefore, and teach all nations, baptizing them in the name of the Father, and of the Son, and of the Holy Ghost: Teaching them to observe all things whatsoever I have commanded you: and, lo, I am with you alway, even unto the end of the world. Amen."* Matthew 28:20

We put signs above our doors, "You are now entering the mission field." Then, why are we not experiencing revival? Could it be that we have little or no power, because God knows that we are not pure? As I review my own life and the service I attempted, I am forced to ask,

What could God have done through me if He'd had all of me?

It is always too late to go back! But it is never too late to begin again! Right where you are, why don't you bow your head and receive Jesus Christ as your Personal Savior and Lord?

Admit that you have sinned against God and ask Him for forgiveness.

Believe that the Lord Jesus Christ is the Son of God Who died for you on the cross, rose from the dead, and is Lord.

Call upon Jesus Christ to be your Lord and Savior.

The Bible says, *"For whosoever shall call upon the name of the Lord shall be saved."* Romans 10:13

Pray something like this,

Lord Jesus, I know that I have sinned. I am sorry. I believe that you died on the Cross, that you were buried, and that you rose from the dead three days later that I might have eternal life.

Please forgive me of my sins, and come into my heart and save me now. In your name I pray.

Amen.

Perhaps you are saying, "I know that I am saved, but I have not given Christ my all! You can change that today by repenting and by committing yourself to live a separated life lived for the glory of God.

Perhaps you are asking yourself, "Why is there such urgency? You lived a double-life for twenty-seven years."

You're correct. I presumed upon the Grace and Goodness of God. I also ruined and lost my relationship with my wife, my son, and my daughter. What are you going to have to lose? *"Be not deceived; God is not mocked: for whatsoever a man soweth, that shall he also reap."* Recently, it was pointed out to me that there is no timetable concerning reaping and sowing!

You will remember in the preface that we began our journey together in the city of Budapest. Let's return there. It is fitting that I share with you one more story, and then you can answer the question, "Why is there such urgency?"

I had driven my co-workers to Budapest from which they had an early flight, and I dropped them at their hotel near the airport. All I had to do was make a right turn on the highway to drive back to Romania. I had absolutely *no business* in the city. You see, *this was almost exactly one year before the night I was beaten and thought I was going to die.* Yes, our God is a patient God. He was about to send me a message loud and clear, but I was blind and deaf.

No, I did not turn right. No, I did not get on the highway and go back to Romania. It was early. I drove toward the city. Why? Compelled by sexual addiction and enticed by temptation, I was yielding to the flesh. I recall that it was a very hot night, and there were lots of people on the streets. The traffic was very heavy. As I approached the city, the cars came to a halt. I wanted to get closer to the center of the city, but at this rate, it would take hours. So, I turned down a side street. There were a few women walking the streets in this area, but I kept going. I really did not know what I was doing nor what I was looking for, if anything. Yet, I drove around and around. Finally,

I decided to try to find the main highway home. I did not have my bearings. Up ahead, I saw what appeared to be a main intersection, and I headed toward the lights. I sat there waiting for the light to turn green, lost in my thoughts. When the light changed, I slowly pulled out of this dark side street on to a main six lane highway ... but I *never* made it!

As I was making the left turn, I saw a car speeding toward me, and so I tried to speed up. I made it across the first lane, but as I entered the second of three lanes, I was hit broadside! My glasses flew off my head into the back seat. Broken glass fell around me. I spun around and around, coming to rest in the very middle of the intersection. I do not know how long I was unconscious. I remember seeing the other vehicle, feeling the impact, hearing the screams, and watching my door caving in on me. When I regained consciousness, people were trying to get me out, but they could not. I was trapped! They tried speaking to me, but I did not understand their language. Worse, I was in *excruciating* pain. At that moment, I could not tell if I was bleeding or not, but I knew that I could not move my left arm. I was experiencing sharp, radiating pain in my neck.

When the police and ambulance arrived, I tried to locate my passport.

Finally, I held my passport to the door so they could see that I was an American. Thankfully, they used the 'jaws of life' to pry open the door and get me out.

While they were working to get me out, I thought, "Lord, help me! Forgive me, Lord!" I was weeping, sobbing uncontrollably. I was not thinking of my *physical* state, but of my *spiritual* state. As I looked around, I saw that the hand brake between the driver's and passenger's seat was bent, pointing to the passenger's door. The steering wheel column was bent. The driver's seat was pushed into the passenger's seat. At that moment, all I could think of was how thankful I was that my wife was not with me. She did not always travel with me. A round trip to Budapest was a ten hour drive. The roads were poor. I speculated that had she had been sitting next to me on this occasion, she would have been killed. God was sending me a number of strong messages that night, almost exactly one year prior to my beating in Budapest, but I did not truly repent that night.

The EMTs and police placed a brace around my neck. They slowly lifted me out of the vehicle and put another brace on my upper body. When we arrived at the hospital, no one was in a hurry. They placed me on a stretcher *and just left me in the hallway!* How painful and embarrassing!

Several days later I found out that my vehicle had been totaled! At the time of the wreck, I thought, "Were it not for my weight and physical strength, I would have been *killed.*" While these may have been factors, I now believe that God was attempting to get my attention. He *did* get my attention, at least, for a while. However, without a genuine sorrow to God *because of my sin,* and not having a repugnant attitude *about* my sin, there was not an inward transformation. Only SORROW! I missed my opportunity. How many warnings have *you* ignored? Friend, a car wreck, or worse, could be in your future!

As I have written this book, there have been innumerable nights when I wished that I had just died in that wreck. That is the coward in me. God has made it very clear that I am to stand, speak, and rescue from the dark side of sexual addiction as many who will hear. As I consider the ledger of *my* life, taking inventory of my gains and losses, I am in a position to urge you to not delay!

Jude 22 International Ministries is God's plan. It is not mine. I talk to pastors frequently about the need for this ministry. Most agree that sin in the churches is of epidemic proportions. While pastors have been very slow to embrace this ministry, men and women continue on a path of certain destruction. Bible-believing Christians need to see the world as God sees it. They need to see their church as God intended it to be: a hospital for sinners! The church ought to be a living body, meeting the needs of all people, not with the social gospel, but with the gospel of Christ. He came to save sinners. He ministered to the woman taken in adultery. He healed the blind. He went out *among the people* in order to bring them to His Father. Jude 22-23 is my blueprint! I pray that it will become *yours* as well!

"And of some have compassion, making a difference:

And others save with fear, pulling them out of the fire; hating even the garment spotted by the flesh."

Paul's prayer for the Colossians is what we need today to meet this challenge:

"For this cause we also, since the day we heard it, do not cease to pray for you, and to desire that ye might be filled with the knowledge of his will in all wisdom and spiritual understanding; That ye might walk worthy of the Lord unto all pleasing, being fruitful in every good work, and increasing in the knowledge of God; Strengthened with all might, according to his glorious power, unto all patience and longsuffering with joyfulness;" Colossians 1:9-11.

Oh, that you and I might:

Be filled with the knowledge of His will. Have wisdom and spiritual understanding. Walk a worthy walk.

Please the Lord by serving those in His church. Be fruitful for the glory of God.

Be strengthened by the spirit of God.

Be patient, and longsuffering toward those who suffer with addictions.

Oh, that you and I *"might make a difference"* for the glory of God. Will you help me? Will you *"pull some out of the fire?"* If we don't, *who will?*

I invite you to become a part of Jude 22 International Ministries. If you know someone who would be helped by this ministry, please contact me at:

Central Baptist Church
13910 Minnieville Rd,
Woodbridge, VA 22193
(703) 583-1717
or Gabriel Rivera
(540) 407-1300
Email: gabrielr11354@msn.com

Restoring a Sinner Brother

"Brethren, if a man be overtaken in a fault, ye which are spiritual, restore such an one in the spirit of meekness; considering thyself, lest thou also be tempted. Bear ye one another's burdens, and so fulfil the law of Christ. For if a man think himself to be something, when he is nothing, he deceiveth himself. But let every man prove his own work, and then shall he have rejoicing in himself alone, and not in another. For every man shall bear his own burden. Let him that is taught in the word communicate unto him that teacheth in all good thing," Galatians 6:1-6

Pick Him Up!

The first responsibility of a spiritual believer who seeks to restore a fallen brother is to help pick him up. When a person stumbles, his first need is to get up, and often he needs assistance in doing it. An integral part of church discipline, therefore, is helping a fallen brother get back on his feet spiritually and morally. What do we do instead? We talk him to death. We beat him down. We tell him, "I told you so. Why, why, why did you do it?" All of this is wrong and is contrary to the Word of God.

Responsibility for the discipline of those who stumble, as well as for those who commit more serious sins, rests on the shoulders of church members **who are spiritual. Spiritual** believers are those walking in the Spirit, are filled with the Spirit, and are manifesting the fruit of the Spirit. By virtue of their spiritual strength, they are responsible for those who are fleshly. They are not the ones who can't wait to shoot the wounded! This is a good test of who's who!

It should be noted that, while maturity is relative, depending on one's progression and growth, spirituality is an absolute reality that is unrelated to growth. At any point in the life of a Christian, from the moment of his salvation until his glorification, he is either **spiritual**, walking in the Spirit, or he is fleshly, walking in the deeds of the flesh. Maturity is the cumulative effect of his times of spirituality. Any believer, at any point in his growth toward Christ likeness, can be a **spiritual** believer who helps a sinful believer who has fallen to the flesh.

The spiritually and morally strong have a responsibility for the spiritually and morally weak. "We who are strong," Paul says, **"We then that are strong ought to bear the infirmities of the weak, and not to please ourselves."** (Romans 15:1). **Spiritual** believers are to **"Now we exhort you, brethren, warn them that are unruly, comfort the feebleminded, support the weak, be patient toward all *men.*"** (1 Thessalonians 5:14).

It is not that **spiritual** believers are to be suspicious and inquisitive. Those are hardly qualities of spirituality. Rather, they will be sensitive to sin whenever and wherever it may appear within the Body, and they should be prepared to deal with it as God's Word prescribes. Both the sinner and the restorer need to feel a sense of brokenness!

There are lots of sex addicts and other guilty individuals not yet discovered or exposed. Each represents an opportunity for a spiritual believer to respond *as Jesus did.*

When the scribes and Pharisees brought to Jesus the woman caught in the act of adultery, they reminded Him that the Law of Moses which required that she be stoned to death. Instead of replying, Jesus bent down and began writing in the sand - perhaps listing sins of which those in the crowd were guilty. **"And the scribes and Pharisees brought unto him a woman taken in adultery; and when they had set her in the midst, They say unto him, Master, this woman was taken in adultery, in the very act. Now Moses in the law commanded** us, that such should be stoned: but what sayest thou? This they said, tempting him that they might have to accuse him. But Jesus stooped down, and with his finger wrote on the ground, as though he heard them not. So when they continued asking him, he lifted up himself, and said unto them, He that is without sin among you, let him first cast a stone at her. And again he stooped down, and wrote on the ground. And they which heard it, being convicted by their own conscience, went out one by one, beginning at the eldest, even unto the last: and Jesus was left alone, and the woman standing in the midst. When Jesus had lifted up himself, and saw none but the woman, he said unto her, Woman, where are those thine accusers? Hath no man condemned thee? She said, No man, Lord. And Jesus said unto her, *Neither do I condemn thee: go, and sin no more.'"* (John 8:3-11).

This woman was shocked and humiliated. Her life of sin had been exposed. I identify with this woman, for I, too, would be shocked and humiliated at the revelation of my sin to my family, friends, and ministry co-workers. With glassy eyes, I searched for someone like my Savior who would not condemn me, but who would restore me.

Please notice that Jesus was not interested in destroying the woman, but wanted to help her. That should be the attitude of His followers toward other people, including fellow believers.

Jesus' command, **"Judge not, that ye be not judged,"** (Matthew 7:1) is often used by Christians to oppose discipline in the church and is sometimes quoted by outsiders who opposed the church taking a strong stand against certain evils. However, as the context makes it clear, (see vv. 3-5), Jesus was talking about a self-righteous, condemning person who acts as judge, passing sentence on others. He only sees the best in himself and the worst in everyone else. If such a person confesses and is cleansed of his own sin, the Lord went on to say, he is then qualified to confront his brother, not to condemn him, but "to take the speck out of [his] brother's eye" (v. 5). He is then **spiritual** and has both the right and the obligation to help his brother overcome a **trespass**.

A pastor once commented, "I have often thought that if I ever fall into **trespass,** I will pray that I don't fall into the hands of those critical judges in the church. Let me fall into the hands of barkeepers, streetwalkers, or dope peddlers, because church people would tear me apart with their long, wagging, gossipy tongues, cutting me to shreds." This is sad, but true.

To restore literally means to mend or repair. It was used of setting a broken bone or realigning a dislocated limb. That is the figure used by the writer of Hebrews when calling on believers, **"Wherefore lift up the hands which hang down, and the feeble knees; And make straight paths for your feet, lest that which is lame be turned out of the way; but let it rather be healed."** (Hebrews 12:12-13).

Spiritual believers first **restore** a fallen believer by helping him *recognize his sin as a sin.* Until a person admits his sin, he cannot be helped out of it. Once he has done that, he must be encouraged to confess his sin before God and turn away from it in repentance, sincerely seeking God's forgiveness.

Restoration of fallen brothers and sisters is always to be done **in a spirit of gentleness,** which is characteristic of those who walk by the Spirit (Galatians 5:23). A Christian who is *critical* and *judgmental* as he attempts to "help" a fallen brother does not show the Grace of Christ. He cannot help his brother, but instead, he may stumble himself.

From the caution **considering thyself, lest thou also be tempted,** it is clear that even **spiritual** believers can stumble. They are made of the same stuff as those who have fallen. They, **too,** could be **tempted** and even fall into the same sin for which they disciplined a brother.

The attitude of every Christian should always be the attitude of Jesus. When a believer needs to help discipline a fallen brother, he should ask and pray for a special portion of Christ's love and gentleness. If the Father does not want even one of His own to be devastated (Matthew 18:14), and if **"For the Son of man is not come to destroy men's lives, but to save *them.*"** (Luke 9:56), how much less do His followers have the right to be destructive rather than helpful?

I desperately needed *someone* to pick me up. I was alone. The pain of my sin caused me to contemplate suicide. When I was asked how I was doing, I lied. I did not want to admit what I was really thinking. I know now that it was Satan and his demons seeking my total destruction. Satan never desires that a child of God be restored. Satan knows he cannot steal us away from the Lord, so he attempts to ruin our lives. He'll even try to kill us if that is what it takes. *I said that I was fine, but I was not.* The fact that my pain was self-inflicted did not negate the Scriptural command to those who are spiritual to restore me.

Hold Him Up

The second responsibility of a spiritual believer who seeks to restore a fallen brother is to help hold him up once he is back on his feet. It is not enough simply to help him turn from his sin and then leave him alone. Immediately after a spiritual victory, Satan often makes his most severe attacks on God's children.

Saying, "I am praying for you," is not enough when a brother or sister is experiencing self-destructive thoughts or even a demonic assault. This is not to *minimize* the power of prayer. Prayer is *only the beginning.* Minutes became hours, hours became days, and days became weeks. We need to physically leave the pulpit and get out of the pew to carry the burdens of one another. I do not believe that "I am praying for you" is what Paul has in mind. There is more, so much more, that needs, to be done.

Christians are to continually (present tense) **bear one another's burdens. Bear** has the thought of carrying with endurance, and **burdens** refers to heavy loads that are difficult to lift and carry. It represents any difficulty or problem with which a person has trouble coping. In this context, the reference suggests burdens that tempt a sinning believer to fall back into the sin from which he has just been delivered. A persistent, oppressing temptation is one of the heaviest **burdens** a Christian can have.

To be freed from a sin is not always to be freed from its temptation. The spiritual believer who truly loves his brother and sincerely wants to restore him to a walk by the Spirit must continue to spend time with him, and make himself available for counsel and encouragement. Prayer is the most powerful weapon believers have in conquering sin and opposing Satan. Nothing helps a brother carry his **burdens** as much as prayer for him and with him. I learned this in my own experience. The Lord brought alongside me a pastor who called me, prayed with me, had coffee with me and put a $100 bill in my hand to be sure that I could meet my needs. He still is walking with me!

The brother who has been delivered from a trespass has an obligation to let his spiritual friends help him carry his burdens. It is not spirituality, but pride that makes a person want to "go it alone." I know how I felt. I know that this is true. However, it is very difficult for a fallen brother or sister to *trust* anybody, or believe that they will accept you unconditionally. There is also a sense that you *are* alone. You sinned, and only you can fix this situation. This is true especially if you have been in a position of leadership. *I need to prove to my church, my wife, and my friends that I can do this.* You are ashamed, broken, and feel unworthy of another's fellowship. Before a leper is received he must first be cleansed!

Strong as he was in the Lord, Paul himself was not free from temptation or discouragement. He confessed that *"For, when we were come into Macedonia, our flesh had no rest, but we were troubled on every side; without were fightings, within were fears. Nevertheless God, that comforteth those that are cast down, comforted us by the coming of Titus; And not by his coming only, but by the consolation wherewith he was comforted in you, when he told us your earnest desire, your mourning, your fervent mind toward me; so that I rejoiced the more."* (2 Corinthians 7:5-7).

When believers bear one another's burdens, they fulfill the law of Christ. Jesus said, "A new commandment I give unto you, That ye love one another; as I have loved you, that ye also love one another." (John 13:34). The law of Christ is the law of love, which fulfills all the rest of God's law.

"For if a man think himself to be something, when he is nothing, he deceiveth himself," (Galatians 6.3). At first glance, that statement seems somewhat out of place. Nevertheless, in light of the call for spiritual believers to restore sinning brothers "in a spirit of gentleness" (Galatians 6.1), the need for such a warning becomes apparent.

One of the chief reasons many Christians do not bother to help fellow Christians is that they feel superior to sinners. They consider themselves to be spiritually **something,** when the truth is that they are really **nothing.** Their desire is not to help a stumbling brother, but to judge and condemn him. At best, they leave him to "stew in his own juice," thinking, if not saying, "He got himself into this mess; let him get himself out." This is terrible, but true. It is very wide-spread. No single group has a monopoly on it. Ask ten pastors to estimate the percentage of those who think this way in their own ministry.

Conceit can coexist with outward morality, but it cannot co-exist with spirituality. In fact, conceit is the ultimate sin, first on the list of things God hates (Proverbs 6:16-17). The Christian who **thinks he is something when he is nothing** needs help in facing his own sin before he can be qualified to help anyone else out of a sin. First, he needs to "take the log out of [his] own eye" (Matthew 7:5). If he refuses to see his own spiritual need, **he deceives himself** and is useless in serving God or in helping fellow believers. The Greek verb behind **deceives** means "to lead one's mind astray" and relates to subjective fantasies that are self-deceptive. This was proven in my own life. Over time, I convinced myself that I had what was merely a besetting sin. I would repent according to I John 1:9, *"If we confess our sins, he is faithful and just to forgive us our sins, and to cleanse us from all unrighteousness."* God is faithful. He would forgive me, I would serve Him, and then sin once again. You see, my emphasis was on listening to what everyone was telling me, rather that hearing and making application of God's Word to my own life. *It really got to the point that I was playing a game!* Sin, then confess, followed by a time of blessing, and then sin again. Much like the children of Israel in the book of Judges.

Repentance, blessing, falling away, God's judgment, and repen-tance. Conceit is one of the devil's subtle tools. Before you know it, you are relying upon your gifts and natural abilities, rather than the Spirit of God.

A believer's first responsibility is to examine himself, in order to be sure his own attitudes and his life are right in the eyes of the Lord, before he ever attempts to give spiritual help to others. Then, and only then, will he have reason for boasting *in a proper way.* There are some burdens that we can share with others, but there are also some that we alone can carry. To avoid my own responsibilities while seeking to help another, is to sin. There must be the spirit of meekness as we seek to help others, not thinking that we are better than they.

We must let God do the judging and the rewarding. He never makes a mistake.

Build Him Up

The third responsibility of a spiritual believer who seeks to restore a fallen brother is to help *build him up.*

Share conveys the basic idea of sharing *equally.* Paul is talking about mutuality, not of one party serving or providing for the other. Both parties share together. The one who is taught the word and the one who teaches have a common fellowship and should share all good things together.

The sharing of all good things is the third step in the restoration of a fallen believer. The spiritual Christian who has picked up and held up his fallen brother also builds him up in the Word. The Word represent the good things in which they fellowship. There's nothing better than the Word of God for spiritual health and healing.

Hope

By Dr. Brad Weniger, Pastor
Central Baptist Church Woodbridge, Virginia

"Why art thou cast down, O my soul? and why art thou disquieted in me? hope thou in God: for I shall yet praise him for the help of his countenance." Psalm 42:5

I am pleased to be Gabriel Rivera's pastor, his brother-in-Christ, and his friend.

I can clearly remember when I first spoke with Gabe after his sin of viewing internet pornography had been discovered. Yes, I can remember it as if it were yesterday. Let me tell you at that point he had hit bottom and had lost all HOPE. What a tragedy! And the story might have ended there, but we love happy endings! (I believe that many of you who are reading this also love happy endings, don't you?) Although his story is far from over, I am thrilled with the day by day progress made thus far by Gabriel Rivera. For this we give God all the glory!

So let me tell you this true story. I promise it will encourage and bless you, and it will give hope to some of you who don't believe there's any more hope in your future because of your horrible past and challenging present.

When Gabe told me of his moral failure, I told him, "There's Hope!" And I meant it.

True rehabilitation (or recovery, if you prefer) from sexual addiction requires Divine intervention. Let that last statement sink in. Self-efforts apart from God (all your "bootstrap religion") may produce some kind of temporal results which resemble authentic change. However, genuine transformation only occurs by God's grace and for His glory. I believe that the Judgment will expose much "wood, hay, (and) stubble" (1 Corinthians 3:12) which our humanistic methods have produced in the field of human improvement.

Sexual addiction isn't simply a case of bad behavior (nor even a case of lots of extremely bad behavior, for that matter). Sexual addiction is a much deeper issue of the soul lacking normal intimacy with God. It is Satan's counterfeit, and it is ironic that the author of confusion would love for all supposed treatments for this aberration to minimize or to avoid spiritual solutions altogether! Furthermore, non-spiritual approaches to sexual addiction offer No Spiritual Hope!

The very goal of the Bible – based counselor is to give hope to the one receiving counsel, making certain to base it on The Truth. "…Rightly dividing the word of truth." (2 Timothy 2:15) and "a word fitly spoken" (Proverbs 25:11) are some of the divine tools with which God has entrusted to us in our calling to "lift up the fallen" (words from the hymn, "Rescue the Perishing").

For over forty years, we've earned a reputation for "taking in" an assortment of prodigals, strays, as well as the wounded and hurting (some self – inflicted). This is not because we have a messianic complex. On the contrary, it is because we have a great Messiah! Never get too far from Hebrews 4:12 – 16:

"For the word of God is quick, and powerful, and sharper than any twoedged sword, piercing even to the dividing asunder of soul and spirit, and of the joints and marrow, and is a discerner of the thoughts and intents of the heart.

Neither is there any creature that is not manifest in his sight: but all things are naked and opened unto the eyes of him with whom we have to do.

Seeing then that we have a great high priest, that is passed

*into the heavens, Jesus the Son of God, let us hold fast our
profession.
For we have not an high priest which cannot be touched with
the feeling of our infirmities; but was in all points tempted like
as we are, yet without sin.
Let us therefore come boldly unto the throne of grace, that we
may obtain mercy, and find grace to help in time of need."*

Briefly stated, this precious Scripture is enough to motivate us
to continue doing as Jesus Christ Himself did, reaching out to the
woman at the well, to the woman taken in adultery, and even to the
thief on the cross, offering hope to those who are otherwise hopeless.
Oh, the indescribable exhilaration which that once – hopeless soul
experiences when we give them real hope. Picture Jesus Christ meeting Simon Peter on the shore in John 21 and saying to the depressed
and backslidden disciple that he could "get back into the game" and
serve the Lord again if he loved the Lord supremely. No other man –
made stipulations. I love that! Peter came away with hope.

However, it is a serious mistake to conclude that successful
counseling is simply making the counselee feel better, even if the
"counsel" which is given is untrue (or, at least, not the whole truth).
The Bible – based counselor must "speak…the truth in love" (Ephesians 4:15). His integrity in fulfilling his ministerial responsibility
will be rewarded by God honoring His own Word (Isaiah 55:11).

So, just what is hope? Chambers Dictionary of Etymology
traces the word from old English "hopa" from about the year 1000 A.
D. More than a mere wish, then it meant trust. Donald K. Campbell,
President Emeritus of Dallas Theological Seminary agrees, saying,

"In casual conversation the word hope conveys a desire or even
a fantasy that is uncertain of fulfillment. Doubt is attached as if the
hope or wish will probably not come to pass. Thus Luke 23:8 states
that Herod "hoped" to see Jesus perform a miracle, and according to
Acts 24:26 Felix 'was hoping' Paul would give him a bribe. The word
hope is only rarely used in this way in Scripture; most often it conveys the meaning of a confident or certain expectation."

Ponder that. "A confident or certain expectation."

When then-pastor Gabriel Rivera was discovered to be guilty of viewing on-line pornography, his whole world came crashing down around him. In time, he would experience total despair. (And the clinical definition? You guessed it: "The complete loss of hope.")

Gabe needed somebody to do for him what God, the Holy Spirit, does for us. The Paraclete cares enough to come along side of us and to tell us the truth, because He is God, He is both supreme love and absolutely righteous.

Gabriel Rivera sent a letter confessing that he had fallen to what he termed as "his besetting sin" (because that's what he thought it was). But it was much more.

Other pastors received that same letter. Now, I know neither their thoughts nor their responses. Without a doubt, some pastors must certainly have prayed for Gabe, for his family, and for his church. Perhaps, some judged him and wrote him off as just another statistic, a product of these last days.

However, the truth is that I don't have to answer for others. Yet, I do know what God told me to do. Without delay, I called Gabe, spoke with him, prayed with him, and very soon we met in person to talk. All I know is that if I had not taken specific, positive steps when I did, I would have been sinfully disobedient. I could not stand in my own pulpit and preach on "the Good Samaritan" had I "passed by on the other side" as did the priest and the Levite in Luke 10.

By the way, some of Gabe's critics have vainly attempted to discount the sincerity of his repentance because he was discovered by others rather than first coming forward himself voluntarily to confess his sin. While such voluntary confession is commendable, it is rare, and lack of it hardly constitutes grounds for judging Gabe's sincerity. Remember the prophet Nathan "culling out" King David with those chilling words, "thou art the man" (2 Samuel 12:7)? Was David not sincerely repentant in Psalm 51? Of course he was! How foolish are these Pharisees who with man-made traditions and rules try to categorize and qualify discipline by God! You see, the actual reason for sinners failing to come forward in voluntary confession is "the deceitfulness of sin" (Hebrews 3:13). We are easily taken in by our own sin! Fooled. That explains it.

Our goal then is not to see how many fallen we can expel, but, rather, how many we can restore through the ministry of the Word of God. What a blessing to hear them pray,

"And now, Lord, what wait I for? my hope is in thee."

Deliver me from all my transgressions: make me not the reproach of the foolish." (Psalm 39:7, 8).

And it is worth it all to see their joy when the Lord says to them, "For I know the thoughts that I think toward you, saith the LORD, thoughts of peace, and not of evil, to give you an expected end." (Jeremiah 29:11).

Psalm 42:5 says, " ... Hope thou in God," not in a system, nor in a plan, rather, God wants the fallen to be restored and to find hope in the person of Jesus Christ Himself (Colossians 1:27).

If I can help somebody as I pass along, If I can cheer somebody with a word or song.

If I can show somebody he is traveling wrong, Then my living shall not be in vain.

If I can do my duty as a Christian ought, If I can bring back beauty to a world up-wrought,

If I can spread love's message that the Master taught, Then my living shall not be in vain.

Then my living shall not be in vain, Then my living shall not be in vain, If I can help somebody as I pass along, Then my living shall be in vain. *(If I Can Help Somebody* by Alma Androzzo.)

DOUBLE-SOUL

Highlights from the Overcomers Victorious Handbook

There are many good recovery programs. Overcomers Victorious is just one. Founded in the 1980's by Dr. Brad Weniger, here are some highlights used with his permission and blessing.

Let's define "Addiction" (a clinical definition).

An addiction is a compulsive or physical dependence upon a substance or person or behavior that provides *a temporary sense of well-being.*

The gratification derived from indulging in an addiction never lasts long, but the destructive effects, the damage to relationships, the feelings of shame and failure that addiction brings are long-lasting and far reaching.

Addictions include:
- Drugs and Alcohol
- Nicotine
- Food (compulsive overeating, bulimia)
- Sex (outside of marriage, abnormal, pornography)
- Work and Success
- Control
- Money (overspending, hoarding, gambling)
- Approval (the need to please people)
- Rescuing Behavior
- Dependency on Toxic Relationships

- Physical Illness (hypochondria)
- Exercise, Diet, and Physical Conditioning
- Perfectionism
- Cleanliness and Avoidance of Contamination
- Obsession with being Organized and Structured
- Materialism (obsession with acquiring things)
- Preoccupation with Entertainment (video, computers, movies, music)
- Obsession with Physical Beauty (cosmetics, sun tanning, clothes, style, cosmetic surgery)
- Academic Pursuits and Excessive Intellectualizing
- Religiosity or Religious Legalism
- Others

The list is long! Everybody, then, knows somebody who is addicted, and everybody could potentially be addicted to something.

The effects of your addiction:
- Physical Health - your body
- Mental Health - your mind
- Emotional Health - your emotions
- Spiritual Health - your soul and spirit
- Financial & Material Well-Being - your money and possessions
- Vocational Stability - your job and career
- Family & Relationships - others who are important to you
- Legal Standing - your freedom

Not to mention your reputation.

Your addiction is not your main problem.

What is *behind* your addiction is your main problem.

You have three enemies who wish to destroy you by using the effects of your addiction against you. Who are these three enemies???
- The World
- The flesh
- The Devil

Life is filled with challenges, difficulties, problems, and heart-aches.

For as long as we can remember in the past, and for as long as we shall live in the future, we have faced and will continue to face life's challenges, difficulties, problems, and heartaches either on the basis of the **TRUTH** or on the basis of **ERROR**.

Truth vs. Error - which is it?

By **TRUTH**, we mean
1. The absolute truth of the Word of God, the Bible, and
2. Jesus Christ, Who is the Truth.

By **ERROR**, we mean

The lies, the half-truths, and the distortions from the world, the flesh, and the devil.

Error says God doesn't care, can't help/won't help us, and we'll never measure up.

Don't buy into the lie that we are unlovable, unacceptable, and hopeless failures with no reason to try.
- Life lived on the basis of error results in poor decisions.
- Life lived on the basis of error results in false identities (masks).
- Life lived on the basis of error is a downward spiral.

The truth is, in Christ we are loved, accepted and victorious.
Some verses to memorize:

"And they overcame him by the blood of the Lamb, and by the word of their testimony, and they loved not their lives unto the death." Revelation 12:11

"Nay, in all these things we are more than conquerors through him that loved us." Romans 8:37

"But thanks be to God which giveth us the victory through our Lord Jesus Christ." Philippians 4:13

Overcomers victorious is effective because of the truth.

"And ye shall know the truth, and the truth shall make you free." John 8:32

- The Truth of Personal Salvation
  Have you established a personal relationship with the God of the Bible by receiving Jesus Christ as your personal Saviour?
- The Truth of Submission
  Have you totally surrendered to God in every area of your life, and do you yield to God as you discover His Will in the Word of God?
- The Truth of Service
  Are you committed to service for the Lord through the local church? There is no way to fulfill God's purpose for our life apart from this.

Overcomers victorious is effective because of the principle of "one another" accountability, the Buddy System.

1. Attend every Overcomers Victorious event that is scheduled.
2. Study the Scriptures daily (with Bible, notebook, and pen and pray, personally applying the truth of salvation, submission, and service in the local church.
3. Stay in continual contact with the Lord and at least one other to whom you are accountable.

Payback

We can never repay the Lord, but when we have been delivered, we should invest in the lives of others, helping them to realize victory through Christ.

"...when thou art converted, strengthen thy brethren." Luke 22:32b

- Be on call 24/7 (the buddy system)
- Bring new ones to Overcomers Victorious
- Give to Christian rehab programs

The program is helpful, but the program is NOT the answer.
Only the Jesus Christ of the Bible can satisfy you.

Jesus Saves, Keeps, and Satisfies!

Other Programs (if they help) may be classified as "good", "better", or "best" depending upon how much absolute TRUTH is foundational in them.

Remember: If there is any truth, it came from God and His Word first! PROGRAMS THAT HELP provide:

1. Mutual support
2. The opportunity to listen to the stories of others and learn from their experience
3. The opportunity to confront those who are in denial or otherwise hurting their own recovery
4. The opportunity to learn about addiction and its causes
5. The opportunity to gain insight into one's own issues and motivations
6. The opportunity to work through one's own resistances and penetrate one's own denial
7. The opportunity to express and ventilate emotion
8. The opportunity to become involved in helping others

Note that a *Christian* recovery group has all of these eight dynamics, plus one more: A fellowship with Jesus Christ at the center

Do not settle for anything but the TRUTH!

Do not listen to friends or family who may not have your best interest at heart.

Do not make excuses!

Excuses

1. You say, "It's impossible."
   God says, "All things are possible." Matthew 19:26
2. You say, "I'm too tired."
   God says, "I will give you rest." Matthew 11:28 – 30
3. You say, "Nobody loves me."
   God says, "I love you." John 3:16, I John 4:19

4. You say, "I can't go on."
   God says, "My grace is sufficient." 2 Corinthians 12:9
5. You say, "I can't figure things out."
   God says, "I will direct your steps." Proverbs 3:5, 6
6. You say, "I can't do it."
   God says, "(You) can do all things." Philippians 4:13
7. You say, "I'm not able."
   God says, "(I) am able." 2 Corinthians 9:8
8. You say, "It's not worth it."
   God says, "It will be worth it." Romans 8:28
9. You say, "I can't forgive myself." God says, "I forgive you." I John 1:9
10. You say, "I can't manage."
    God says, "I will supply all your needs." Philippians 4:19
11. You say, "I'm afraid."
    God says, "(I have) not given you the spirit of fear." 2 Timothy 1:7
12. You say, "I'm worried and frustrated."
    God says, "Cast all your cares on me." I Peter 5:7
13. You say, "I'm not smart enough."
    God says, "I give you wisdom." I Corinthians 1:30; James 1:5
14. You say, "I feel all alone."
    God says, "I will never leave you nor forsake you." Hebrews 13:5

Remember, God is there for us in everything! It's not about how capable you are --- it's how great God is! Unknown

God loves you!

He desires for you to know that you are accepted by Him through His Son Jesus Christ.

He wants you to embrace the security that is yours in His Son Jesus Christ.

He calls out to you over and over in His Word that you are significant to Him because of His son Jesus Christ.

He has given us His Word to build you, guide and strengthen

you. Every day spend time in His Word meditating upon the
following affirmations:

DOUBLE-SOUL

Who Am I in Christ?

I Am Accepted in Christ

John 1:12	I am God's child
John 15:15	I am Christ's friend
Romans 5:1	I have been justified
I Corinthians 6:17	I am united with the Lord and one with Him in spirit
I Corinthians 6:20	I have been bought with a price; I belong to God
I Corinthians 12:27	I am a member of Christ's Body
Ephesians 1:1	I am a saint
Ephesians 1:5	I have been adopted as God's child
Ephesians 2:18	I have direct access to God through the Holy Spirit
Colossians 1:14	I have been redeemed and forgiven of all my sins
Colossians 2:10	I am complete in Christ

I Am Secure in Christ

Romans 8:1, 2	I am free forever from condemnation

Romans 8:28	I am assured that all things work together for good
Romans 8:33, 34	I am free from any condemning charges against me
Romans 8:35	I cannot be separated from the love of God
2 Corinthians 1:21	I have been established, anointed and sealed by God
Colossians 3:3	I am hidden with Christ in God
Philippians 1:6	I am confident that the good work God has begun in me will be perfect-ed
Philippians 3:20	I am a citizen of heaven
2 Timothy 1:7	I have not been given a spirit of fear, but of power, love and a sound mind
Hebrews 4:16	I can find grace and mercy in time of need
I John 5:18	I am born of God and the evil one cannot touch me

I Am Significant in Christ

Matthew 5:13, 14	I am the salt and light of the earth
John 15:1, 5	I am a branch of the true vine, a channel of His life
John 15:16	I have been chosen and appointed to bear fruit
Acts 1:8	I am a personal witness of Christ's
I Corinthians 3:16	I am God's temple
2 Corinthians 5:17–20	I am a minister of reconciliation
2 Corinthians 6:1	I am God's coworker

Ephesians 2:6	I am sealed with Christ in the heavenly realm
Ephesians 2:10	I am God's workmanship
Ephesians 3:12	I may approach God with freedom and confidence
Philippians 4:13	I can do all things through Christ who strengthens me

Taken from Living Free in Christ, by Neil Anderson

Friend, you do not have to remain broken. God is willing, I dare say waiting to put the pieces of your life back together for His glory, if you would but come to Him in repentance. May this devotional from Mrs. Charles Cowman, Streams in the Desert, March 15 encourage you.

DOUBLE-SOUL